Domestic Violence and the Church

Domestic Violence and the Church

Helen L. Conway

paternoster
press

First published 1998 by Paternoster Press

Paternoster Press is an imprint of Paternoster Publishing,
P.O. Box 300, Carlisle, Cumbria, CA3 0QS, U.K.
http://www.paternoster-publishing.com

04 03 02 01 00 99 98   7 6 5 4 3 2 1

British Library Cataloguing in Publication Data

A catalogue record for this book is available from the British Library.
ISBN 0-85364-817-4

This book is printed using Suffolk New Book paper which is 100% acid free.

Cover design by Forum Marketing, Newcastle-upon-Tyne
Typeset by Design2Print, Droitwich, Worcs.
Printed in Great Britain by Clays Ltd., Bungay, Suffolk

For Dennis

Contents

Acknowledgments

A portion of this book is based on the thesis I wrote for my M.Phil. degree at the University of Cambridge, so thanks is properly due to those who assisted with that original work, including my supervisor Dr. David Farrington. Especial thanks, however, is due to my parents, David and Marcia Conway, who gave sacrificially to fund me through that degree and without whose support this book would never have materialized.

Thanks also to my best friend, for keeping me sane and smiling when deadlines were pressing; to St Helens Women's Aid, who taught me much about the work of their organization; to members of the Knowsley Domestic Violence Forum who taught me about their organisations and the value of inter-agency co-operation and to those victims and clients who have shared their stories with me and given me the understanding to write this book.

Credit is also due to my husband, Dennis Woodcock. He gained mention in the original thesis, when he was just a friend, for 'his patient identification of my typing errors'. His patience and talent as a proofreader continue and are now supplemented by large doses of encouragement, support and food and drink delivered to the study on a regular basis. Without him I would have dehydrated!

Introduction

Jimmy was a short, agitated man who squirmed in his prison seat as I spoke to him. An ordinary Liverpudlian electrician in his mid-thirties, he gave me my introduction to domestic violence. He was remanded in custody in Walton prison on a charge of assaulting his wife. As a student on a work placement in a solicitor's office I was there to take a further statement from him.

> 'There's nothing more to tell you,' he said. 'We had an argument – it was about the gas bill of all things. She was irritating me and I just slapped her across the face in temper. I did say I was sorry. It was just a normal lover's tiff. Nothing to justify all this.'

He gestured at the locked door with a work-calloused hand. His wife's injuries, disguised in the medical terminology of the doctor's report lying on the table in front of me, did sound mild.

Later, at the trial, the prosecuting barrister passed me a set of photographs of Jimmy's wife's injuries, taken at the hospital on the night of the assault. One eye was swollen shut, her face a mass of deep bruising. Her lip was split, one tooth broken into a jagged edge. Her hair was matted from the blood which had seeped from a head wound. Yet, worst of all, was the pain in her eyes as she looked into the camera. Her gaze was full of betrayal and hopelessness.

Since then I have progressed through various studies to qualify as a solicitor specialising in family law. In my own office I have had women from all walks of life tell me how their most intimate relationships were shattered by violence from their lovers' hands.

These people who approach me represent just a tiny fraction of the families throughout this land who are suffering from domestic violence. This issue is one which is fast moving to the forefront of society's concerns. The laudable efforts of concerned journalists and campaign groups have made domestic violence topical. And yet it is not a new problem. There are many indications that violence has occurred in families – usually by men against women – throughout many centuries and in various cultures.

An ancient Chinese proverb says, 'A woman married is like a pony bought – to be whipped at the master's pleasure.' Similarly, a traditional Serbian saying instructs, 'Beat a woman and a horse every three days'. Punch, the traditional English children's character who beats his wife Judy, in fact derives from a Roman mime called 'Marccus'. Even in classic British literature, the problem of domestic violence appears – the Shakespearean character Petruchio says of his wife, 'I will be master of what is mine own: She is my goods, my chattels.' (*Taming of the Shrew*; act 3, scene 2).

It is probable, therefore, that domestic violence has occurred in families throughout history. However, it has only been since the seventies, when Erin Pizzey set up the first women's refuge at Chiswick Women's Aid, that any serious research has been done into the issue. Since then interest in the subject has continued to grow, both in the UK and abroad – most notably in the United States.

This book aims to give an introduction to the issues surrounding domestic violence from a Christian perspective. It is hoped that it will be of assistance to a wide range of readers who may encounter domestic violence in different ways: victims or their friends and relatives, pastors, social workers, doctors, counsellors and so on. I seek not only to give readers an understanding of what it is like to live with domestic violence and how victims are affected, but also to raise questions about how the church can respond to the issue.

Chapter 1 explains just what domestic violence is, whilst

chapter 2 answers some of the common questions about domestic violence, such as who may be affected and why victims endure violence for so long. Chapter 3 then looks at these issues from a theological standpoint. What does the Bible say about violence in the home? What guidance does it give on how the church should respond?

Chapter 4 examines the causes of domestic violence. It looks at the various theories put forward and shows how these can be intertwined to produce a fuller picture. This chapter puts the theological teaching into a more practical setting.

Chapters 5 and 6 look at the social and legal sources of help open to victims in order to equip the church to direct victims to forms of assistance which the church itself cannot supply. Chapter 7 then looks more closely at the philosophies behind these sources of help, showing how the traditional emphasis has been on facilitating the victim's escape from the violence. Chapter 8 proposes a more appropriate response – seeking to eradicate the violence. Finally, chapter 9 suggests how, armed with all this information, the church can practically assist in dealing with domestic violence both on an individual and a social level.

Much of the theoretical side of this book has arisen out of research I did for theses at the Universities of Hull and Cambridge. However, it was only as I began to work with victims, assisting them to gain legal protection, that I really began to understand the subject. The examples used in this book are all real, although in all cases names and identifying details have been changed to protect client confidentiality. In some cases two stories have been combined into a composite example. According to the statistics mentioned later in this book, it is likely that each reader knows several people who have experienced domestic violence, although that violence may not be common knowledge. The aim of this book is to equip readers and the church to start to consider a compassionate and effective response to such victims.

One

What is Domestic Violence?

So just what is domestic violence? In the week before I began to write this chapter I saw three clients, all of whom had different experiences, but all of whom I would say were victims of domestic violence.

Karen was married to James. Over a seven-year period he had hit her on many occasions, causing broken bones and bruising.

Stephanie was living with Clive. He had hit her only once – a short slap on the cheek whilst they were on holiday. When they returned she terminated the relationship. He then started a campaign of harassment which lasted for months. At first, he refused to leave her flat. Before he finally did leave, he smashed it up. He bombarded her with unwanted gifts and letters and tried everything to persuade her to take him back. He would visit her late at night, drunk and uninvited. He would watch her house, later letting her know that he was aware exactly how long her visitors had stayed.

Joanne had three children by her partner Tom. He was often rude and abusive to her and had a habit of keeping her awake all night, refusing to let her sleep. One night, in front of friends, he called her derogatory names and held a bottle in her face, threatening to kill her. Her friends helped her to escape by taxi whilst he continued to threaten her. As she left, he pushed their daughter onto the pavement. She felt that the children were at risk and decided to leave. He refused her access to their clothes and belongings and they ended up in a temporary homeless hostel with the children dressed only in their pyjamas.

As these few examples show, domestic violence is not a concept which is easily defined. It may be regarded narrowly, using terms such as 'wife battering' or 'spouse abuse' to confine it to the context of physical violence between adult parties. Other studies have looked at domestic violence in the wider context of the family unit as a whole, including violence aimed specifically at children or the increasing problem of 'elder abuse'.

There is no doubt that violence can extend to all interpersonal relationships. However, this book concentrates on abuse between spouses and cohabitees and the effect of that abuse on the children of those relationships. The reasoning behind this particular focus is that the wider the definition, the wider the range of issues which need to be addressed. For example, sexual abuse of children is commonly treated by professionals as a different area from 'domestic violence'. 'Elder abuse' involves issues concerning the role and care of elderly people within our society which do not touch on violence between spouses.

Even the term 'violence' carries differing connotations. Some researchers have placed the emphasis on the use of some degree of physical force. Others look at the motivation behind the physical act. For example, Leonore Walker's definition of domestic violence, for the purposes of her study:

> . . . is a woman who is repeatedly subjected to any forceful physical or psychological behaviour by a man in order to coerce her to do something he wants to do without any concern for her rights.[1]

---

[1] Walker, Leonore, *The Battered Woman* (Harper Colophon 1979)

In this book a much wider definition of violence is used.
Indeed, violence covers all kinds of physical abuse: kicks,
punches, slaps, pushes, burns, use of weapons, pulling hair,
shaking, dragging, choking, biting, rape and so on.
However, it is most important to recognize the mental
component of domestic violence. Domestic violence is
closely linked to control and manipulation of the victim by
the perpetrator and there are a whole range of ways he can
accomplish this without resorting to a physical assault. All
of these ways, however, override the rights, desires and
emotions of the victim.

The victim may be intimidated by the destruction of
property, the display of weapons or generally aggressive
actions. Threats of violence can be as frightening as the
violence itself, particularly when the victim knows the
perpetrator may carry out the threats. In some cases the
pattern of violence is preceded by seemingly
inconsequential actions which the victim knows are the
precursor to violence. These very actions can be used to
control a victim. For example, one woman who sought help
from a Liverpool counselling agency said that her husband,
when he became angry, would click a ballpoint pen on and
off, on and off, on and off. In time she learnt that this was
a warning sign of violence to come and so his switching the
pen on and off would cause her to respond as if he had
actually inflicted the violence.

Verbal abuse of victims is extremely common. Constant
use of filthy and derogatory terms – often sexual in nature
– demoralize a victim, making her feel worthless, dirty and
unloved. Such verbal abuse can result in the victim coming
to see herself in those terms. She may believe that she is
such a bad person that she actually deserves the violence,
or such a stupid person that she cannot cope alone. The
verbal abuse, therefore, serves to control the victim and to
compound the effects of physical violence.

Victims can also be controlled by isolation. Constant
questioning of her movements or control of her reading
material or friendships are all forms of control over the
victim. Other perpetrators may use the children as a tool to
control her – threatening that if she leaves he will gain

custody of the children or harm them if she does not do what he wants. One man would 'persuade his wife to consent' to sexual intercourse against her will by threatening that if she did not go to bed with him he would do it anyway – in front of the children. Abuse can also be economic – keeping the victims short of money or deliberately getting the family into debt. Some abusers humiliate victims by making them account for every penny they spend and criticizing their choices. A particularly humiliating form of economic abuse is to withhold money for sanitary protection.

The personal accounts of victims of domestic violence in chapter 2 illustrate how this emotional abuse is an integral part of domestic violence and must be included in the definition used here. Indeed, some would prefer to use the term 'domestic abuse' rather than 'domestic violence'. However, since the latter is the most commonly used phrase, 'domestic violence' is adopted in this book.

Can men be victims?

Research on domestic violence was initiated mainly by feminists and the focus remains mainly on women victims. The Law Commission report of 1992 stated:

> Nearly all studies have shown that in the great majority of cases, men are the perpetrators of domestic violence and women are the victims.

Certainly the high-profile media coverage of domestic violence has all featured women victims – such women as Sara Thornton and Kirinjit Allawallia – abused women who eventually killed their husbands – or soap opera *Brookside* character Mandy Jordache. However, the focus is now slowly shifting as recognition grows that men may also be victims. An article by Victoria Freedman in the *Irish Times* (13 February 1995) cites the example of Les Davidson, who in 1994 set up a helpline for male victims.[2]

---

[2] Freedman, Victoria, in Donnellan, C. (ed) Violence in the Family (Cambridge; Independence 1995) p.24

A further article by Victoria McDonald in the *Sunday Telegraph* (January 1995) mentions a seven-month study of 'battered men' carried out by Sean Stitt and Audrey Macklin of John Moores University in Liverpool.[3] The researchers thought that there would be only a small number of cases and found themselves 'surprised and horrified' by the numbers of male victims they found. Audrey Macklin's Ph.D. dissertation (1995) entitled 'Battered Husbands: The Hidden Victims' concludes:

> It is absolutely apparent from this research that anyone can be a victim of domestic violence, no matter how old, what class, whether employed or in what type of employment, and most importantly any gender.

There are many reasons why the problem of male victims is not commonly recognized. Male victims are not always as visible as female victims, having more economic power and thus being more able to leave and start again without assistance from aid agencies. Society as a whole is less willing to accept male victims, and there are fewer services to which male victims are able to turn for help. If a victim is not going to gain anything by admitting the violence, he is unlikely to speak about it. When interviewed by Victoria McDonald, Sean Stitt said that the social workers they spoke to:

> '...adopted an ultra loony feminist argument of men getting a taste of their own medicine. They had a totally sniggering attitude towards our research.'[4]

In light of the research which has been done, it must be accepted that men can be victims of violence. However, there is still a lot more research needed before we can know if there are as many men as women who are victims and whether the same issues arise in the cases of male victims. For these reasons, this book refers throughout to the man as the perpetrator and the woman as the victim. However,

---

[3] McDonald, Victoria, 'Battered husbands afraid to seek help', in Donnellan, C. (ed) Violence in the Family (Cambridge; Independence 1995) p.23
[4] ibid.

the reader should bear in mind that the roles can be reversed. The arguments and recommendations set out in this book apply equally to male victims insofar as the issues involved are the same. It should also be remembered that the church is as responsible to male victims as to female victims.

How common a problem is domestic violence?

There are several reasons why it is impossible to obtain a completely accurate picture of how widespread the incidence of domestic violence really is. It is all too easy for domestic violence to remain a hidden crime, known about only by the parties involved. By definition it will take place primarily behind closed doors. Victims often feel misplaced shame or guilt at being a victim. Some are constantly told by their abusers that they bring the violence upon themselves, and eventually this message becomes internalized. Others are so isolated or are amongst friends and family who do not have a realistic view of domestic violence and have no one in whom they can confide. Thus, many incidents of domestic violence remain a secret.

Since different pieces of research use differing definitions, figures are bound to vary from study to study. For example, a study asking about only physical violence may well come up with smaller numbers than a study which also encompasses threats and other verbal abuse. Other studies are skewed because of the methodology used. Some statistics rely on data collected by the police. There are several ways of logging a domestic violence incident – as just that, as an assault, as a breach of the peace or as a no-crime, for instance. If the violence is not ever brought to police attention or the victim does not follow up by pressing formal charges, the figures will not accurately reflect the true level of domestic violence in society.

Thus, it seems that the statistics are more likely to be on the low side than on the high side. Nevertheless, as the following statistics show, there is a frighteningly high level of domestic violence in our society.

■ One survey was carried out by a market research company in 11 towns in Great Britain in August and September 1989. A sample of 1,007 married women were approached in the street: 33 per cent said that they had experienced violence in their marriages. Twenty-one per cent had been threatened with violence. Of those women who were now divorced or separated, 46 per cent had been threatened and 59 per cent had been hit by their husbands.[5]

■ The British Crime Survey in 1992 estimated that half of all offences of violence against women involved domestic violence. The same survey estimates that only one-fifth of all incidents of domestic violence are reported to the police.

■ Every year, Women's Aid England provides help and refuge for around 30,000 women and children escaping domestic violence. A further 100,000 are given help and support.

I have not yet managed to discover a study of the incidence of domestic violence among church members in the UK. Indeed, that is one of the primary reasons for this book, since it is often the case that general awareness of the problem must be heightened before more in-depth study will be commissioned. However, this is not to say that the church in the UK remains aloof and unaffected by the problem. The church is the body of Christ, not in heaven but on earth, and as such ought to be concerned and responsive to issues which occur in our modern society. The statistics above clearly illustrate that there is a large number of people – for they are people and not merely statistics – suffering from domestic violence, to whom the church should be ministering.

Further, the lack of British research mirrors the pattern of research into the incidence of domestic violence in

---

[5] Painter, Kate, 'Wife Rape in the United Kingdom' – Paper presented at the American Society of Criminology 50th Anniversary meeting, 20-23 November 1991, San Francisco

society as a whole. It is by no means unusual for criminological research to commence in the United States and then for its results to be reflected in further work in Great Britain. Domestic violence statistics are remarkably similar in both countries. Similarly, practical measures to deal with the problem – such as court-mandated therapy for offenders – have frequently started in America and then been imported and adapted to Britain.

It is relevant, therefore, to look at recent evidence from America to see whether it is likely that domestic violence may occur within the church. The most striking study is that done by James Alsdurf and Phyllis Alsdurf, now published in the UK in their book Battered Into Submission.[6] Apart from several personal accounts of victims who were church members, they also report on their own research programme.

The Alsdurfs sent a questionnaire to five thousand Protestant pastors throughout the US. One-third of those who responded came from Assemblies of God and Independent Baptist denominations. The remaining two-thirds represented thirty-one other denominations. Less than ten per cent of those provided with a questionnaire actually responded, which may well be an indication that church leaders currently have an apathy to this issue which needs to be shaken.

Of those who did respond, four fifths indicated that they had confronted wife abuse in the ministry and had counselled a woman who had been physically abused by her husband. One-third of the pastors had counselled six or more women. Three-fifths of them had counselled a victim during the six months immediately preceding the questionnaire. Of course, these figures are likely to be an underestimation of the true incidence of domestic violence in the church since not every victim will reveal it to the pastor.

US churches which are addressing the issue are finding their efforts met with a great demand. A report on the

---

[6] Crowborough, East Sussex, (Highland 1990)

Internet[7] states that the Mennonite Central Committee has now produced four packs dealing with family abuse. Two are on sexual abuse, one is entitled 'The Purple Packet – Domestic Violence Resources for Pastoring Persons'. Another pack on domestic violence called 'Lord Hear Our Prayers' was added in 1994. An estimated 17,000 copies of the first three packets had been sold by January 1994, making them top MCC sellers second only to popular cookbooks.

Churches in the New Bedford area are also beginning to offer a personal, community-based response to domestic violence.[8] In this traditionally Catholic area the bishop offers his priests information on domestic violence. Education about domestic violence is also a part of marriage preparation classes. At the local Catholic Social Services, nine staff members offer counselling for couples and families. The incidence of domestic violence is so high that one of the staff members, Maria C. Pereria, has a caseload specifically geared to violence in the home. In 1994 she saw one hundred and seventy-four cases, sixty-five of which were into violence defined by the centre as 'heavy duty stuff – assaultive behaviour'. In the same community a Baptist minister, Dr Edgar Stone, director of the Interfaith Counselling Centre, stated, 'We see a number of clients who are victims of abuse. In fact I'd say seventy-five per cent had some sort of violence involved in their histories'.[9]

The fact that no-one has yet funded a specific research programme into UK churches does not mean that the problem does not exist. It may, however, be an indication of the lack of knowledge about the issue within the church which this book seeks to resolve. If 33 per cent of women suffer violence, the church should be concerned. If those women come into the church as a result of outreach programmes to victims, they will come in still suffering from domestic violence – or the aftereffects if they are no

---

[7] http://www.mennonitecc.ca/mcc/pr/1994/01-28/4.html
[8] http://www.ultranet.com/newstandard/projects/domviol/spiritual comfort
[9] ibid

longer in the abusive relationship. To pastor and care for these women effectively, the church must be aware of the issues involved.

Jenny Daggers, writing in the Interdisciplinary Journal of Pastoral Studies 'Contact' says:

> The issue of domestic violence is a microcosm of the wider feminist challenge to Christianity, one which provides an uncomfortable focus on an extreme outworking of the structural sin of sexism. Women's pain and anger need to be received by the whole community of Christian women and men.
>
> . . . Borrowdale sees the vital Christian project to be a critique of masculinity and of distorted relationships between the sexes, to enable a restoration of the shared image of woman and men in God . . . Lee envisages the church as a place where non-violent, nurturing relationships between men and women are developed.
>
> I would draw together the concerns and visions of these writers by envisaging the church as a renewed community, where women and men practise together new relations of mutual respect and nurture with sharing of power and responsibility . . . . Commitment to this renewal indicates a practical, communal way of building up the body of Christ...
>
> The challenge to the Christian community and to pastoral theology to develop a relevant pastoral response to battered women exists at all levels from the individual to the societal.[10]

In other words, the church has a duty to respond to individual victims of domestic violence, be they within or without the folds of the church. It also has a duty to address the causes and effects of domestic violence within society. The aim of this book is to inform the church in order that it can begin to respond to this challenge.

---

[10] Daggers, Jenny, *Interdisciplinary Journal of Pastoral Studies 'Contact'* 116 (1995) pp. 3ff

Two

Domestic Violence – The Reality

Some people dismiss the concept of domestic violence as a figment of the feminist's fevered imagination, a tactic to allow knickerless man killers such as Sara Thornton to 'get off' with their crimes. Others see it as a source of fun – the cartoon image of Flo chasing Andy Capp with a rolling pin. For others it is a fact of life, an acceptable way of controlling a spouse and no cause for complaint. Then, for the victims and those who support them, domestic violence is something else altogether. It is a pernicious, evil force which has seemingly destroyed the potential of their lives.

Domestic violence is still a largely misunderstood phenomenon, surrounded by popular myths, which hinder or prevent the assistance which should be given to victims. Statistics show that a victim makes on average, between five and twelve attempts to obtain help before she finds an appropriate and supportive response. This situation may well be due to a lack of knowledge and understanding on the part of the potential helpers. This chapter aims to discuss some of the basic questions surrounding domestic violence and to correct some of the common myths.

Who is abused?

It is a myth that only low-income women are abused. It is a myth that abuse only happens in 'problem families'. It is a myth that it only happens to housewives. It is a myth that it does not happen if the extended family is close. It is a myth that it only happens to young women. In fact, it is a myth to say anything other than that domestic violence can happen to all women, everywhere, as the following personal accounts show. These stories are largely (although not exclusively) drawn from my own experience as a family solicitor and represent just a tiny fraction of the type of suffering which is, even now, occurring behind the closed doors of our own communities.

Carole's husband was manager of his own packing company. The family home, worth in the region of half a million pounds, was located in a picturesque village. Carole enjoyed the village social life – an au pair helped her care for her two daughters. Her husband Tom put long hours into the company, eventually winning various business awards. Carole said of him, 'He was always highly motivated, aggressive in his approach, always striving for improvement.' However, as the recession began to bite, he found himself under more and more pressure at work, and his aggression ceased to be channelled solely into his marketing strategies. He began to bully his family and to insist on perfection in everything – even from the two pre-school children. When the family failed to live up to his demands he used violence. The first occasion came as a shock. He pushed Carole into a bookcase with the baby still in her arms. She put this violence down to the pressure of work but it continued with punches to the head and body. On one occasion he smashed her two front teeth with his fist.

The final straw came one day when she was leaving home for her tennis club. He returned from work earlier than expected, demanding a meal. When she refused to let her tennis partner down he snatched the tennis racquet from the passenger seat of her Mercedes. As she sat behind the wheel he systematically smashed all the windows of the car, then dragged her out of the car by her hair. It was only the arrival of the au pair that stopped him. She took the children away that night and in the morning sought legal help.

Hannah was in her seventies when she first came to see me. She had two adult sons and had actually divorced her husband Harry some five years previously. However, his bullying behaviour was such that he had prevented her obtaining financial independence and so they still shared the same house.

Throughout the marriage he had systematically demoralized her, telling her over and over again that she was 'only a housewife with a little hobby' despite the fact she was a highly trained nursing manager. She was assaulted on many occasions, each time hiding the bruises or telling colleagues that she was clumsy and had fallen or bumped into things. He refused to let her keep her own earnings despite the fact that for much of the marriage she was the sole bread winner. He would give her a small allowance which was never really enough. He refused to let her use the washing machine, telling her to wash her clothes by trampling them underfoot in the shower as he did. He would measure the amount of water she put in the washing-up bowl, only allowing her exactly one and a half inches no matter how many dishes there were. A woman with tremendous personal dignity despite her mistreatment, she tried to escape his clutches by continuing to do as much charity work as she could once she had retired. Her health deteriorated, and when I met her she was registered as disabled and at high risk of stroke and heart attack. Still he would not drive her to the shops, forcing her to carry heavy bags the three miles from town to the house. She only sought help when she saw her daughter-in-law being treated the same way by her own son:

> 'I hid it all from everyone for my children and then my grandchildren,' she said. 'As I was brought up you just didn't wash your dirty linen in public – even now the neighbours don't know I am divorced. I didn't want my sons to know what their father is like – they love him. But now I know I deserve better. I put up with it because I thought that was the right thing to do. Now they [the children] are doing just the same thing. Is it too late for me?'

It wasn't too late – she is now living in a specially adapted flat, protected by an injunction order.

Surinda is thirty-two and has three daughters:

'I came over from India for an arranged marriage in 1981. I loved my husband a lot and after two years I gave birth to a daughter. That was when the beatings started. Then I had another child – again a girl. There is enormous pressure to have a boy. In Asian families girls are nothing. I had to cope with his family taunting me and calling me 'useless' because I hadn't given him a son. In between all this I had to work in the family shop from 9 am to 11 pm as well as raising two children and cooking for his family. Back home I had a degree but no-one cared about that here. The third baby was born in 1988 – again a girl. For the first six months of her life my husband never even came near her. My life seemed so pointless that I tried to kill myself twice; I was so worn down by his verbal abuse and beating. Soon after, my husband took us all to India on the pretext of a four-week holiday. He went off one day and left us there – no passports, no papers, nothing. He said he'd kill me if I returned to England. Then he went back. We were stranded for two years and only came home because my brother paid for the tickets. When I got back my husband filed for divorce because he wanted a son. I never wanted to associate my name with divorce because in my culture it brings you and your family huge shame. You are treated with contempt; the thinking is that when a marriage fails it is always the woman's fault. Yet it was my husband who was the violent and unfaithful one. We divorced in 1992, and now he is remarried and has a son. I have nothing – no family, no support and no money.'[1]

Mandy was an eighteen-year-old barmaid in a city pub when she met John. He was seven years older and had the reputation among his drinking pals of being a 'tough lad'. Thrilled by his attentions, she commenced a relationship. When she became pregnant just three months later she moved in with him. Her parents expressed their disgust at her morals. 'They actually told me I was a dirty little scrubber,' she said.

Disowned by them, she felt unable to return home when he hit her on just their second night together. Then, about a week later,

---

[1] In Donnellan, C. (ed) *Violence in the Family* (Cambridge: Independence 1995) p.9

he came into the pub where she still worked and saw her smile at a male customer. 'He had just cracked a joke that's all,' she explained. 'It was part of the job to be pleasant – make the punters have a good time. That was what they came in for.' But John didn't see it that way. He came around the bar and dragged her out by her hair, kicking her legs as she tried to resist. The landlady, knowing John's reputation, stood aside. The customers in the bar pretended not to see – not one came to her rescue. At home he pushed her on to the sofa and stood over her, ranting and raving.

'He called me a prostitute and worse. He told me that I was his woman now and I was not for sale for the price of a pint. This was my only sexual partner saying this to me – the man I had loved so much I had lost my family for him.'

When she argued, he hit her repeatedly in the stomach, causing her to fear for her unborn child. He then raped her, 'claiming back what was his'. When he had finished he left again to go to a club with his mates. She spent the night curled on the sofa, not daring to move for fear she would be in the wrong place when he got home. He returned in the early hours then got up to go to work, not saying a word to her.

When he had gone, she went to the local police station. She was forced to explain to a burly uniformed police man what he had done. He then did get a woman PC who explained that it would be almost impossible to get a conviction and that they could not guarantee he would be locked up right away if she pressed charges. Demoralized she returned home. As her pregnancy progressed, so did John's behaviour. He frequently hit her, often with no apparent reason, 'It was like it was a sport to him. Nothing on TV, so hit me.'

After the first occasion he was careful not to hit her stomach but still caused her physical injury, on one occasion breaking her wrist. He frequently sexually abused her, sometimes with instruments. He even threatened to get his mates round to take part, but never did. He would lock Mandy in the house when he went out, only allowing her short trips to the local shops and then questioning her when she returned about whom she had met. 'I had no friends, no family – nothing. It seemed like this was it for the rest of my life.'

Her child was born with severe medical problems. 'I don't know if he did it to her or not but I still blame myself. Whatever the medical causes the stress that baby was under inside me wasn't right'. He came to the hospital with her for the birth – to make sure that it was a female doctor who attended her. Then he was not to be seen again until she came home alone.

> 'When he found out the baby was ill he just looked at me like he was so disgusted I couldn't even do that right. Two weeks later he came home to find me giving the baby medication. He went bananas shouting and screaming that I shouldn't waste my time looking after a little runt. He snatched the medicine off me demanding I cook for him.'

She cooked him a meal. When he went out to the pub, locking her in, she packed a small bag, smashed a window, climbed out and went to the accident and emergency department of the hospital at which the child was treated. She had the child checked and told the female doctor she could not go back. She spent three hours on the plastic seats in the waiting room until the doctor got in contact with a local women's group. They came and collected her, gave her overnight accommodation and then put her on a train to a new city some three hundred miles away. When I met her she was in a refuge, about to be rehoused. She had only what she could get from social services.

As these four stories show, each victim will have a different experience of domestic violence. She will bring to it her own background, her own personality and reactions, and she will be abused by a man who is also an individual being. Some attempts have been made, however, to profile the sorts of women who are likely to be abused. The task is complicated, by the fact that it is almost impossible to distinguish between the characteristics presented by an abused woman as a result of the violence and those which existed before the violence.

Leonore Walker, who has become an authority on the so-called 'Battered Woman's Syndrome', conducted in-depth interviews with 120 battered women. She found that those women frequently:

(a) had low self-esteem

(b) accepted responsibility for the batterer's actions

(c) suffered from guilt yet denied the anger and terror they felt

(d) presented a passive face to the world

(e) had severe stress reactions with psychophysiological complaints

(f) had traditional views about home and family

(g) believed that no-one could resolve the predicament except themselves.[2]

However, her definition of violence for the purposes of the study assumed repeat attacks. It is my experience that many women who have higher self-esteem and confidence are able to approach a solicitor or other source of help at an early stage, perhaps after just one or two attacks. As one woman said:

> 'He hit me once and he said he'd never do it again. I just forgave him. Then he did it again and I told him – once more and he'd lose me. Last night he thumped me again. I'm leaving now before he beats the strength out of me. It's not going to get better. Three times is already worse than none at all.'

The fact that some women are able to get out of the relationship before the violence descends to the bottom of the spiral of repeated abuse does not mean that those women are not affected by the violence. They will still suffer a broken relationship and a loss of hope, they may well have financial difficulties and feelings of deep shame and regret. Different women are affected by domestic violence in different ways, but all are victims.

Who abuses?

Again, the stories above indicate that any type of man can abuse his partner. I personally have dealt with cases

---

[2] Walker, Leonore, *in* Johann, S.L. and Osanka, F. (eds) *Representing . . . Battered Women Who Kill* (Thomas 1989) p. 1701

involving men who were unemployed, a lorry driver, a car mechanic, an accountant, a chemical engineer and a retired further education lecturer, to name but a few. Again, it is a myth that only men earning a low income or men who are not in the professions are abusers.

It is also a traditional but simplistic view that all domestic violence is caused by the abusers being under the influence of alcohol. Many cases do involve substance abuse. A British study published in the *British Medical Journal* found that 74 per cent of abusive husbands had a drinking problem.[3] Other researchers found that various studies noted that between 36 and 52 per cent of wife batterers also abused alcohol.[4] However, the fact that there may be an association between alcohol and violence does not necessarily mean there is a causal connection. The drinking may itself may be a symptom of the underlying stresses or personality traits which are also causing the violence. For example, in Carole's case, Tom began to drink whiskey more often and more heavily at the same time as the violence began. She felt he took refuge in the alcohol to escape the pressures at work. Alcohol did not, in fact, allow him to forget the problems but it did reduce his inhibitions about taking out his frustrations on his family.

Alcohol may also be used, whether consciously or not, as a socially acceptable excuse for the violence. In today's society it is common for men (and women) to drink to excess and not be in control of their actions. So, to be able to claim, 'I don't remember hitting her – I was drunk,' is a convenient way for an abuser to deflect responsibility for his actions. On the other hand, the alcohol may simply diminish the control which an abuser may otherwise have on his temper and make it more likely for independently existing violent tendencies to be exercised. Even where the alcohol has an association or a causal connection with violence, it can be argued that drinking is a socially learned

[3] Gayford, J.J., 'Wife Beating: A Preliminary Survey of 100 Cases', *British Medical Journal* Vol.1 No. 595 (1975) pp. 194–7
[4] Gelles, R.J. and Cornell, C.P., *Intimate Violence in Families* (London: Sage Publishing 1985) p. 72

behaviour – one which is inherent in our culture. Thus, in considering the role of alcohol in domestic violence, there ought to be a consideration of the way society accepts alcohol and places expectations on men to drink.

It is also commonly believed that abusive men come from abusive families. Again, this is a partial truth. The same *British Medical Journal* article mentioned above found that over half of the men in this study had witnessed their fathers assaulting women.[5] Another study of 270 victims found that 45 per cent of their abusers had witnessed parental violence and 37 per cent had been abused as children. Again, there is clearly a potential connection. In further chapters it will be seen that the so-called 'inter-generational transmission' of violent behavioural patterns is a potential – but not exclusive – cause of domestic violence. This transmission theory holds that violence in the home is something which children learn from their parents.

In terms of the characteristics of abusive men, Leonore Walker profiled the battering male, finding him to frequently:

(a) possess low self-esteem

(b) believe in traditional male / female stereotypes

(c) blame others for his actions

(d) feel jealous

(e) present a dual personality

(f) respond poorly to stressful situations

(g) not believe that his violent behaviour should have negative consequences.[6]

Domestic violence is closely linked to control and manipulation. The acts of violence and the abuser's general attitude to the victim are often calculated to place the woman in a subservient position, a position which does not present a threat to that of the abuser or which allows his

---

[5] Gayford, J.J., op. cit
[6] Walker, L., op. cit p. 170

home to be run as he wishes without objections from others. This control is illustrated in the stories told earlier. Thus, this profiling may be useful to understand the motivation behind some of the violence.

A man with low self-esteem and poor stress responses may well feel threatened and vulnerable, either at home or at work. This could well have been a contributing factor to Tom's violence. Violence can be an attempt to regain control and dominance. This may have underlain Harry's abuse of Hannah: she always had a better career and higher earnings than he did. Or violence can be a way of overcoming jealousy as the abuser asserts himself as more influential than those of whom he is jealous – for example, a newborn child, or his partner's family. Certainly, John seemed to have a strong jealous streak. While profiling may explain the motivation behind some of the violence, it is not an infallible way to identify a man who may in the future be violent to a partner. Like victims, each abuser is individual and may come from any walk of life and any range of income, class or age.

Why do women stay in abusive relationships?

Many women do not stay. Some may leave after only one or two incidents of violence. Others may leave after repeated attempts to free themselves from the tangled webs of their lives. However, others stay – either for the present or for the rest of their lives. A common myth is that these women stay because the problem does not really exist. Accusations are made that the woman only complains to gain attention or as a scheme to get the family rehoused. Another myth is that victims stay because they like it, because they gain a perverse form of sadomasochistic pleasure from the violence. In actual fact, there are a plethora of interrelated reasons why a woman may still be living in the shadow of an abusive relationship.

One of those reasons is emotional attachment to the relationship. At some stage in the woman's life there must have been a strong bond of love between the victim and abuser for the relationship to have commenced. This love may still burn strongly in the heart of the victim. Women may look at the superficial causes for the violence and concentrate on those: 'It's only when he drinks.' 'It's just his temper when things are not going too well for him at work.'

Most abusers have other characteristics other than their violent tendencies – the reasons the woman was attracted to him in the first place. If he remains good with the children, generous with money, or witty and amusing in company, the woman can still find herself attracted to him despite the violence.

It is a natural human coping strategy in the face of adversity to search for reasons to hope. Women often invest huge amounts of emotional resources in a relationship, both before and during the violence. She may have given up close family to be with him, or sacrificed her career to care for the family. Or the relationship may have gone through other difficulties and she has had to struggle with difficult compromises to make it work. Having invested so much of herself in such an intimate relationship, the victim may well not want to lose the relationship – just for the violence to stop.

Except in the most severe cases, the violence is not usually constant. Generally there is a cycle which may be relatively long or short, depending on the couple. The cycle will begin with the violent incident. Thereafter it may be followed by the abuser's repentance. This could be genuine, or else calculated to preserve the relationship for his own reasons. He may promise not to do it again. He may say he is sorry and he will get help. He may play on her underlying emotion of love for him, begging her not to leave him. Thereafter, if this repentance is accepted, there will be a 'honeymoon' period, in which the relationship is much happier. However, as time goes on the tension between the parties will build up again until it culminates in another violent incident, followed again by repentance, and so forth. This cycle will continue indefinitely until it is broken by one of the parties.

A woman's decision to leave will most logically be made immediately after the violent incident. This is the time when the wounds (both physical and mental) are the most painful, when the reasons for leaving are most clear. By the time the 'honeymoon' is reached, the last incident can be put to one side and the victim may find it easier to believe that everything will be all right in the future. As will be seen later, the violence itself has psychological effects which will make a decision to leave difficult. At the same time the victim has to contend with the repentance of the abuser which can be manipulative in its effect. An abuser becomes skilful at using the woman's weakest points to persuade her to stay. Thus, the underlying original love for the abuser, the natural instinct of hope and the pattern of violence itself can combine to trap the victim in the relationship.

The victim may also stay out of love for her children. An outsider may feel that the children would clearly be better off outside an abusive family environment. However, the choice is not so easy for the victim who has to weigh up the emotional, financial and educational consequences of taking the children away from their father. Leaving may mean that the children lose out materially – they may have to live in shared refuge accommodation or survive on welfare benefits. To get to a place of safety they may have to move to a new area, causing a change of schools. A mother may feel that her children are better off at home. This is especially so when the abuser is not directly violent to the children. The victim may feel she can put up with the violence to give her children the benefit of a close relationship with their father.

Emotions at the other extreme of the spectrum may also conspire to keep the victim in the relationship. Fear and terror of the consequences of leaving can be powerful motivators. An abuser frequently reinforces his control over the victim by threatening to kill her if she leaves. The abusers tell the victims that they will be found no matter where they go. For many, these are not empty, but distressing, threats. Such warnings have culminated in many incidents of violence and abuse. Some may feel that the 'punishment' they get for leaving will be worse than the present abuse. Some women may even have tried to leave in the past and been forced back by their abusers. Other emotions, such as shame at having to admit to a failed relationship, or embarrassment at the intimate nature of her horrors, may make a victim reluctant to leave since she knows she will have to explain her reasons for leaving to at least one person. To be rehoused she will have to explain why she is now homeless. To prevent her welfare benefits being reduced she will have to tell the Child Support Agency about the violence. To get legal help she will have to tell a solicitor the details. The prospect of all this may simply be too much for a victim.

In addition to these inbuilt emotions, the psychological effects of the violence itself can debilitate the victim. The Women's Aid Federation (England) Research Group wrote in a 1981 report:

> The constant pressures of the violent situation are debilitating. The experience of pain, confusion and humiliation leads to a paralysis which is not easily shed. Beyond the initial confusion, apathy and despair, we noticed a continuing loss of confidence, energies and initiative, an inability to cope with officialdom and difficulty in making decisions.

A woman suffering from such side effects may have the basic will to want to escape the violence but may simply be unable, on her own, to make her desires a reality.

Leaving is not just a question of walking through the front door. It also involves obtaining alternative housing, moving the children's schools, disentangling joint finances and debts and obtaining independent financial resources. Some victims will be married to the abuser and will need to go through a divorce. Victims may have to leave without any possessions whatsoever and have to start again from scratch. Apart from finding the energies to tackle the plethora of official agencies which this may involve, the victim will also need to know where to find help. For a victim who has not even been allowed a say in the running of her own household, finding this help can be a daunting prospect. Unless a victim knows where to find help, she is unlikely to leave.

The theory of 'learned helplessness' suggests that a victim will at first try to modify her own behaviour to prevent the violence . She may notice that the violence seems to occur when she comes back from the sporting activities he takes part in, so she may stop going to them. If the violence continues she may then wonder whether it is because she wears short skirts when she goes out of the house. So, she may switch to wearing trousers. However, she will find that the violence continues. Since the violence is not in fact linked to her behaviour, but rather to the attitudes and beliefs of her abuser, her efforts will have no effect. She will then translate her inability to protect herself into a perception that she has no control over her life. This perception may in turn cause her to believe that there is no point in her leaving, since nothing else she has tried has worked.

An abuser is also likely to place direct pressure on a victim not to leave. Apart from specific threats to her own safety, abusers may use other methods of control and manipulation. Much of this manipulation can be psychological – for example, blaming her for the break-up of the family, rather than accepting that the violence is the real reason. Abusers may use the children, threatening to fight her for residence (custody) if she leaves or warning about the harmful effects if she splits the family. Despite the violence, victims remain incredibly vulnerable to the expressed views of their abusers. It is as if their old self-image has been destroyed by the violence and a new one rebuilt in its place, founded on the negative comments of the abusers. Since this new self-image is reinforced by the cycle of violence and the learned helplessness, the victim can genuinely come to believe that her abuser has the true picture of her character and the effects of her actions.

On top of all these factors, there may be cultural pressures on the victim to stay. She may have been taught that marriage is for life – no matter what. Or she may come from a religious background which stresses the sanctity of marriage and the headship of the husband. The common portrayal in our society of a good mother as one who will suffer for her children may also affect her considerations.

Ethnic minority women may face extra pressures unique to their racial culture. For example, the Newnham Asian Women's Project Annual Report 1993–94 stated:

> Although domestic violence is now widely held as unacceptable in the Asian Community there are many cultural and social pressures that continue to tyrannise women into staying in violent relationships or returning to violent partners. The fear of reprisal is a major consideration for all women seeking to escape. For Asian women the urgency and immediacy of their fear can only be appreciated in the context of the community backlash, which has encouraged and sanctioned the unlawful activities of 'bounty hunters' and other vigilante-style guardians of Asian women's *izzat*. The woman is still believed to uphold not only her own honour but also that of the assailant, the family and the wider community. The shame and stigma of separation and divorce still has a powerful hold on Asian women's lives.

Finally, it is arguable that there is an established institutional confirmation of all these pressures. Generally women in our society are less powerful than men in economic terms. This means that the system collaborates with the abuser in making it harder for the victim to leave the home than it would be for a man. It is not just a question of the victims obtaining new accommodation with their wages. Most women still earn less than men if they work outside the home at all, and so they struggle far more to run a house on their own. Also, the woman is more likely to have the children living with her, and the cost of childcare often militates against the woman's ability to take herself off welfare benefits and earn higher wages.

Women from ethnic minorities who have recently entered the country may even find that the immigration laws militate against them being free to leave an abusive relationship. A report by Southhall Black Sisters, contributed to a Victim Support conference (sponsored by Marks and Spencer) on 23 April 1993, shows how this can happen:

The one year rule requires that immigration applicants remain in marriage for one year before being given indefinite leave to stay in Britain. This rule is racist because it is based on the assumption that people enter marriage to enter this country. There is also an assumption that women enter marriage for convenience, whereas, in all cultures, women enter marriage for fulfilment . . . .

'The one year rule makes women entirely dependant on their spouses, economically, socially, physically and emotionally. They risk being deported if they leave violent relationships before their immigration status is made secure. They cannot claim public assistance (benefits, housing and so on) before their status is settled . . . .

'These women will not go to the police for fear of deportation. In some cases the police, DSS or local authority has reported back to the Home Office on the immigration status of women making complaints.

How are the victims affected by domestic violence?

It is a myth that, once the physical injuries of a violent attack have healed, the victim is left unaffected. Apart from the fact that the worst assaults may leave victims with permanent physical injury, there is also the psychological effect of the violence.

That a victim may be afraid is not a startling statement. However, the effect that fear may have on her may well run much deeper than an outsider would ever guess. The fear will rule all her decisions and actions so that she may get to the stage where even the simple act of choosing a dish for dinner will be coloured by her fear of what he might do if he did not like it. This depth of fear can have a debilitating effect on her physical health. Sleep patterns may be disrupted, causing prescription of and ultimate dependence on drugs. She may also experience other stress-related illnesses. The fear acts as an immobiliser, preventing the woman from developing as she should in the process of her life.

In order to cope with the fear a woman will automatically employ various psychological 'coping facilities'. She may internalise the blame, accepting that it is her fault. The consequent guilt can be a crippling emotion if it is not dealt with appropriately. If her abuser constantly tells her it is all her fault, she will gradually accept this guilt, especially when combined with the learned helplessness mentioned above. Her view of herself will be formed by her beliefs, which are coloured by her abuser's caustic and hurtful verbal abuse.

A woman who is constantly told she is at fault, useless, no good or is referred to in demeaning sexual terms will take a low view of herself out of that relationship when she leaves. This poor self-image is all too easily reinforced by having to live on a low income in shared temporary housing – usually not all she would like for her children. Thus the view of herself as useless and incompetent is reinforced, even in her new life. This low self-esteem will continue to affect her – in forming new relationships, in meeting new platonic friends, in trying to build up a new career to support herself – unless someone can take the time to replace the negative self-image with positive messages.

This problem can be intensified by the isolation into which many victims are forced. The isolation may be directly imposed by the abuser as a part of his overall control. He may seek to prevent her from working or seeing friends. He may alienate those friends she does have by his behaviour. On the other hand, this isolation may come from her own reactions to the violence. She may have overwhelming feelings of shame which cause her to hide herself away. She may withdraw from her social activities when in the early stages of trying to prevent the violence via modification of her own behaviour. Once she is isolated there are fewer opportunities for outsiders, who retain an objective view of her as person rather than just victim, to help her alter her self-view. Isolation can also engender feelings of deep loneliness which can in turn lead to forms of depression.

Domestic violence is not just about the battering of a

body. It is about the systematic destruction of the whole person. It is about the theft of hope and self-confidence and about foisting on victims a skewed perception of themselves as seen from their abusers' own glazed eyes.

What about the children?

It is a myth that children can be effectively protected from the violence which goes on in their own home. Children living in the shadow of an abusive relationship are inevitably affected. Some may suffer violence directed at them – either by the abusive partner or even by the victim, who at the end of her tether vents her anger on the children as a last resort. Even those children who are not physically abused, however, will be affected by just being in the same house as the violence.

NCH Action for Children conducted a survey in their family centres which produced some alarming statistics about those children who have lived through this experience. Seventy-three per cent of women in the survey said that their children had witnessed violent incidents, and 67 per cent said they had seen their mothers beaten. Ten per cent of the mothers were sexually abused in front of the children and a full 99 per cent of them said they had seen their children crying and upset because of the violence. 72 per cent said the children had been frightened, 48 per cent that they had become withdrawn and 34 per cent that they had developed bed wetting problems. 31 per cent said that the children had intervened to protect their mothers. 33 per cent thought that their children had become violent and aggressive and 29 per cent said they had become resentful and embittered. 24 per cent thought that their children had problems trusting people and forming relationships.[7]

Pat Shea, tutor at Liverpool Community College, produced notes for a counselling course indicating a whole catalogue of ways in which children are likely to react to

---

[7] *The Hidden Victims* (NCH Action for Children 1994)

stress. Whilst admitting that any child can be under stress, she emphasizes that children from violent homes are more vulnerable to excessive symptoms of stress such as the following.

Pre-schoolers (birth to five years)

- physical complaints such as stomachache and headaches

- sleep disturbances

- bed-wetting

- whining, clinging, anxiety

- failure to thrive

School-age children (6 to 12 years)

Children in this group may

- become seductive or manipulative as a way of reducing tension in the home

- fear being abandoned

- fear being killed or fear themselves killing someone else

- fear their own anger and other's anger

- exhibit eating disturbances

- become insecure and distrustful of their environment

Boys in this group may begin to manifest aggression, low tolerance and frustration. Girls may withdraw and become passive and compliant, constantly seeking approval.

Adolescents

Adolescence is a particularly stressful stage and that stress becomes even more acute for those teenagers from violent homes. The more extreme of these behaviours may include:

   - escape into drug or alcohol abuse

   - running away from home

   - suicidal thoughts and actions

   - homicidal thoughts and actions

Domestic violence destroys the safe environment of family life in which children should ideally develop. The messages of love and protection which give them emotional stability are shattered because the parents, who are their primary source of physical nourishment and emotional stability, are engaged in bewildering exchanges of violence.

Domestic violence is not an insignificant difficulty faced by a small minority. It is a widespread phenomenon of devastating effect on those who are victims. It is an experience which can scar those involved, both physically and emotionally, for the rest of their lives. It is a social disease which the church has a responsibility to combat. The victims are people to whom the church has a responsibility to bring healing.

Three

What Causes Domestic Violence?

If the church is to respond to the issue of domestic violence it first needs to establish the basis on which it does so. The rest of this book will deal with legal and sociological information and arguments about domestic violence. However, the church's moral authority to become involved stems from the truth and power it possesses as the body of Christ. Whilst individuals within the church may well possess academic or professional qualifications which equip them to become involved in this issue, the church as a body must act from a spiritual, rather than a purely sociological, standpoint. Therefore it is vital that we obtain a theological overview of the issue of domestic violence before moving on to consider its causes and cures.

It is all too easy to acquire knowledge about domestic violence. It is a topic which is coming rapidly to the forefront of current social attention. As a result there are a plethora of textbooks on the subject. However, knowledge alone is not necessarily sufficient to produce a productive response. As Paul said, 'Knowledge puffs up, but love builds up.' (1 Cor. 8 :1) The aim should be to acquire wisdom and understanding which allows the church to translate the knowledge into practice in a manner consistent with biblical principles.

An examination of the Scriptures relating to this issue must be the starting point. As Proverbs 1 :7 says, 'The fear of the LORD is the beginning of knowledge, but fools despise wisdom.' Again in Proverbs 9 :10 it is stated, 'The fear of the LORD is the beginning of wisdom, and knowledge of the Holy One is understanding.' (See also Jb. 28 :28 and Ps. 111 :10.)

Where interpretation and evaluation of evidence is involved, the answer to a question will so often depend on the angle from which it is asked. For example, if an Australian was to be asked which was the coldest month of the year his answer would be different to that given by a New Yorker. Their answers would depend on their general world view. If the church's response to domestic violence is to be consistent with Scripture, then its initial analysis of the situation should come not from a feminist or criminological stance. The church must ask as its very first question, 'What light does God's word shed on the issue, and what response does the Word of God demand?'

However, Scripture must also be the culmination of our understanding. The New Bible Commentary says that the Hebrew word for 'beginning' in Proverbs 1 :7 is *r'esit*. The word implies both a starting point and an essence. Any information gathered in a search for understanding and wisdom must be continually measured against the standards of God in order to grasp its true meaning. Such a complete theological overview will provide a general framework into which any criminological or sociological information later acquired can be fitted.

A woman who has just suffered a beating at the hands of her husband may ask herself what she has done wrong to cause the violence. She may well look at her own behaviour or personality to find the cause of his behaviour. Perhaps if she had only cooked a better meal or if she had not let the children be so rowdy in their play the attack would not have happened. Perhaps she somehow provoked her husband into being violent.

A psychiatrist dealing with a violent spouse may look into his background to see if there were any elements of his upbringing that may have caused his violent tendencies. Did his father hit his mother? Was he abused himself as a child? On the other hand, a probation officer dealing with a man convicted of assaulting his wife may look at his personality traits. Does he evade responsibility for his actions? Does he have a learned pattern of violent behaviour which needs altering?

A sociologist may look at the environment in which the a buse took place. Was it caused by stress in the family – perhaps because of poor living standards or recent unemployment? Is there alcohol or drug abuse in the family, or a history of mental illness which may be a contributing factor? A criminologist may look at the wider social setting. Does violence occur because the criminal system is too soft on domestic violence and there is no effective sanction against it? Does it happen because violence is accepted generally within our society and it just trickles down into the family setting?

On the surface, there is no one simple answer to the question, 'What causes domestic violence?' Various theories have been put forward, each reflecting the initial stance taken by those seeking to answer the question. Some place blame on individuals, some on family background and others on society as a whole. We will look at these theories in more detail in the next chapter, when we will also see that no one theory can produce a definitive answer to the question. However, we will see that if the theories are all combined in a certain way (producing a 'combined causation model') then, together, they produce a better picture of what causes domestic violence. It is as if each theory is a weak ray of light which cannot fully illuminate the issue. These rays are weak because they are limited by the way the question is approached. Each theory has been developed by people with differing world views – for example, the so-called 'patriarchal theory' was developed mainly by feminists. However, if the theories are combined the weak rays combine to shed more light on the situation. Even this combination, however, does not provide a complete answer. It is only when we add to the studies the teaching of the Word of God, which acts as a lamp to our feet, that the whole answer can more clearly be seen.

The Bible provides a one-word answer. What is the cause of domestic violence? Sin. Sin is essentially a spiritual concept, speaking of a wrongdoing which causes a separation from God. Isaiah 59 :2 states, 'But your iniquities have separated you from God; your sins have hidden his face from you, so that he will not hear.' The Bible also speaks of the concept of original sin. Sin, having been passed down the human line from Adam, has become endemic in our society. Sin now exists in society as a general force which affects each human from birth. As the psalmist said, 'Surely I have been a sinner from birth, sinful from the time my mother conceived me.' (Ps. 51 :5).

It would be oversimplistic, however, to merely state that sin is responsible for domestic violence and take the question no further. Several questions remain: what causes a particular sinful act or situation to become so embedded in our society that it becomes acceptable? Why is sin manifested in domestic violence in certain families but not in others? The church needs to understand how Satan traps people into a sinful behaviour pattern if it is to seek to change that behaviour. The Bible uses military analogies in its description of the church's fight against evil in the world.

> Put on the full armour of God so that you can take your stand against the devil's schemes. For our struggle is not against flesh and blood, but against the rulers, against the authorities, against the powers of this dark world and against the spiritual forces of evil in the heavenly realms. (Eph. 6 :11–12).

A team of soldiers told to attack a particular target would not just move in upon receiving their mission statement. An advance group would be sent in to gather intelligence. The soldiers would want to know the types of weaponry stacked against them. They would want to know the areas in which the enemy was active to ensure they covered all the occupied ground. They would then assess the tactics likely to be used by the enemy and would come up with the best method of countering those tactics. When they had all the information available to them, had evaluated it and placed it firmly in the context of their own goals and capabilities, then, and only then, would they be ready to attack. Likewise, the church must have a full picture of the issue of domestic violence before it seeks to move in and deal with the situation. The Bible teaches that Satan is a cunning schemer and we need to be alert to his plans (2 Cor. 2 :11; Acts 20 :31; 1 Pet. 5 :8).

The next chapter deals with the 'combined causation model' and shows that belief systems and societal norms come together to produce an environment in which domestic violence is both produced and nurtured. There is nothing in this model which shows that any one factor forces an abuser to use violence. However, the model does indicate how a mindset is produced which allows the violence to appear rational and acceptable to the abuser. The duplication of this mindset in many individuals means that the violence becomes a part of what is normal in society as a whole. Once this normalization happens, it becomes harder to challenge the violence. An incident of domestic violence ceases to be a wayward act, becoming instead one which is fairly typical of the behaviour of many members of that society. Thus, fewer and fewer people become outraged when they learn of an incident of domestic violence, and so fewer people are inclined to act against it. Society becomes apathetic and accepting of spouse abuse.

Validity can be given to the argument that sin is the cause of domestic violence by an examination of the biblical concept of sin. Harper's Bible Dictionary (p. 955) defines sin as 'that which is in opposition to God's benevolent purposes for his creation.' Therefore, to assess what is sinful it is necessary to have a full understanding of God's purpose for his creation. In order to assess what is wrong about domestic violence it is necessary to know his plan for the family.

The Bible gives no comprehensive list of sinful actions. Rather, there are plenty of examples of how sin manifests itself in given acts or beliefs. However, it is clear that violence is condemned in the Bible as a product of sin.

Right at the beginning, God made it clear that violence was contrary to his plan for the world. Shortly after the account of the fall of man, Genesis 6 :11 reads, 'Now the earth was corrupt in God's sight and was full of violence.' Ps. 11 :5 reads, 'The LORD examines the righteous, but the wicked and those who love violence his soul hates.' Ezekiel spoke of God's attitude to violence: he was angered by it – 'Must they also fill the land with violence and continually provoke me to anger?' (Ezk.8 :7) – and wanted an end to it. 'Give up your violence and oppression and do what is just and right'(Ezk.45 :9)

It is also clear that violence within the family unit is condemned. In Obadiah 10 the Lord says, 'Because of the violence against your brother Jacob, you will be covered with shame; you will be destroyed for ever.' The book of Obadiah deals with the feud between the tribe of Edom and Israel, Edom being the descendants of Esau, Israel the descendants of Jacob. Bringing the matter right back to its family roots, God reminded the people of their duty to family members. As Matthew Henry's commentary points out, in Old Testament theology there was a duty to be a *goel* – a redeemer – to your family. It was particularly abhorrent, then, that there should be violence within the context of a relationship that should be a protective one. God also proclaims his distaste for family violence in Malachi 2 :16, a verse which will be examined below.

These verses all refer to physical violence. However, we have already seen that damage can also be done by verbal or mental violence. These forms of violence are also condemned in Scripture, as in Proverbs 10 :6,11: 'Blessings crown the head of the righteous, but violence overwhelms the mouth of the wicked...The mouth of the righteous is a fountain of life, but violence overwhelms the mouth of the wicked.' James also warns about the destructive powers of the tongue, in chapter 3 :6,8, 'The tongue is also a fire, a world of evil among the parts of the body... no man can tame the tongue. It is a restless evil, full of deadly poison.' A desire or a love for violence' whether or not it is acted upon is also condemned. Proverbs 13 :2 says, 'From the fruit of his lips a man enjoys good things, but the unfaithful have a craving for violence.' In his Sermon on the Mount Christ taught that even contemplating a sinful act is as bad as committing the act itself (Mt. 5 :21,22, 27,28).

There are several words used in the Bible to denote sin. None of these words refer to specific actions. Rather, they all indicate a particular state of mind or a concept relating to the ultimate effect of a given action. Bob Gordon, in his book *Foundations of Christian Living,*[1] provides the following list of words for sin which is divided into four main sections.

(i) Deviation from a norm or a standard

> *Chattah:* to miss the mark or go wrong (Jud. 20 :16, Ps. 51 :4)

> *Avon:* to bend or pervert, i.e. deliberately do what is wrong even though you know what is right (Jb. 33 :27)

> *Shagah:* to go astray or err (Jb. 19 :4, Lv. 4 :13)

> *Parabasis* (NT): swerving from a straight line, i.e. transgressing over a boundary (Rom. 4 :15, Gal. 3 :19)

> *Hamartia* (NT): to miss the mark (Mt. 1 :21, Rom. 6 :23)

> *Paraptoma* (NT): to trespass, take a false step in contrast to a true one or fall off a path (Col. 2 :13, Eph. 2 :5)

(ii) Description of a state

Sin is a fixed state in which men are trapped.

> *Rasha:* often translated as 'wicked' or 'ungodly' (Ps. 1 :6; 37 :28)

> *Asham:* to offend or be guilty (Gn. 26 :10, Lv. 5 :15,16, used of a guilt offering)

---

[1] Gordon, B., with Fardouly, D., *Foundations of Christian Living* (Chichester: Sovereign World, 1988) pp. 11,12

(iii) Deliberate rebellion

This is a state where people feel they can cope without God i.e. in pride people declare their independence from him.

> *Persha:* to shake the fist at God (Is. 1 :2, 1 Ki. 12 :19)

> *Anomia* (NT): lawlessness or rebellion (2 Cor. 6 :14, 1 Jn. 3 :4)

(iv) Devious actions or attitudes

> *Marah:* to be contentious, rebellious or stubborn (Ps. 78 :8)

> *Marad:* to rebel (Nu. 14 :9)

> *Ra'ah:* to be evil or bad, i.e. a specific act of evil (Gen. 19 :7)

It is the absence or existence of one of these states of mind or attitudes – a 'conceptual sin state' – that determines whether an act is holy or sinful. This is well illustrated by the gospel accounts of the temptation of Jesus – see Matthew 4 :1,11.

The temptations commenced after Jesus had been fasting for a considerable time. Satan's first tactic was to suggest that Jesus should use his powers as the Son of God to turn stones into bread. It was not sinful per se for Jesus to use his inherent miraculous powers. However, the essence of this temptation was that he should misuse his powers to assuage his own hunger. Those powers had been given to him to bring glory to the Father, and to use them for his own satisfaction would have been *hamartia*, to miss the mark – to use the powers incorrectly. Also, it was no accident that Jesus was hungry – he had been led to the desert to fast by the Spirit. To circumvent the testing time by misusing his powers would also have been *persha*, to 'shake his fist at God'.

The second temptation was to use the angel's protection, referred to in Psalm 91. Clearly, there is nothing sinful in claiming the promises given in Scripture. However, in this context it would have been a perversion of the meaning of those promises. Jesus' knowledge of Scripture enabled him to see that Satan quoted the psalmist out of context and thus avoided the sinful attitude of *avon*, to bend or pervert. The temptation here was, in essence, to launch himself as Messiah by a spectacular sign, which was not in God's plan. If Jesus had done so he would also have been guilty of *paraptoma*, to take a false path.

The third temptation was to bow down and worship Satan in return for the kingdoms of the world and their splendour. There is nothing wrong in being in a position of worldly rulership. Godly men have frequently been placed in positions of political power. Indeed, it could have been thought that the political power to rule over all these kingdoms would give Jesus the opportunity to put into place all the principles of the kingdom of God by civil, legal or political measures. However, the first problem here was how this would be achieved. To switch allegiance from God the Father to Satan would have been *anomia* – the lawlessness or rebellion in 2 Corinthians 6 :14, where it is specifically stated, 'Do not be yoked together with unbelievers. For what do righteousness and wickedness have in common?' Also, Jesus was not sent to be a political king – a ruler with only an influence of a lifetime, a ruler whose principles could only be established by coercion over his subjects. To accept Satan's offer would have meant that he failed to fulfil his role as eternal Saviour by dying on the cross and thus, would have been *shagah* – to go astray or err.

From the temptations of Jesus it can be seen that Satan tried to trap Jesus by getting him to slip into a sinful attitude. Jesus was able to detect the fallacies in Satan's arguments because of his knowledge of Scripture. Had he not had this knowledge and had he not had a true sense of his own destiny and the will of his Father, then the devil's suggestions would have seemed plausible and acceptable.

The same need for knowing Scripture applies to the issue of violence. The Bible does show situations where violence is not condemned. It is used in the wars fought by the Israelites when they were establishing their position in the promised land. It was used by Jesus when he cleared the temple area of merchants and money changers (Jn. 2 :12ff.). In these and similar incidents, the violence was not sinful because it fell in with God's purpose. It was a legitimate use of force. The general condemnation of violence applies to situations where that violence is not in accordance with divine purpose but is instead used for man's own ends. A full knowledge and understanding of Scripture is needed to distinguish between those situations where violence is permitted and those where it is not.

The account of Jesus' temptations also shows that Satan will use half-truths in his efforts to tempt someone into sinning. For example, Satan could simply point out an expensive watch lying unattended and suggest to someone that they steal it. Most people would reject such a suggestion. However, if half truths are used, the temptation becomes more difficult to resist. Satan may suggest that the Bible teaches that the rich should not hoard wealth and that the loss of the watch would not harm the owner. He may say that the Bible teaches that the rich should help the poor and since the person being tempted is poor, it would be God's will for him to have the watch. He may even use the argument defeated by Paul in Romans 6, saying that even if it is a sin to take the watch, God would forgive the thief anyway. It is as the person being tempted is able to outweigh these half-truths with a conviction based on the full truth – the complete teachings of the Bible – that the temptation will be resisted.

As the combined causation model is discussed in the next chapter, it will become apparent that many of the elements in that model involve skewed biblical principles. In other words, Satan has made half-truths rather than full truths the general basis for behaviour within our society. The result is that whilst some of the patterns of behaviour which contribute to domestic violence are partly good, they are in fact 'just off the mark' that mark being the standards which God sets for the good of his people.

For example, one element in the combined causation model is 'inter-generational transference'. This theory argues that domestic violence is a pattern of behaviour which is passed down from parents to children who observe or experience domestic violence in their upbringing. The children learn that behaviour from their parents. Teaching children and bringing them up to emulate parents is commended by the Bible. Proverbs talks of 'training a child in the way he should go'. However, when parents teach children something which is not biblical they are missing the mark; they are sinning. We will see in the next chapter how this sin becomes embedded in society. For example, men are conditioned that it is their role to bring up male children as men, not to let their sons become 'sissies'. Therefore, a son may be taught that Dad, as the man of the house, is to be respected. If hitting Mum is the way to achieve that respect, then the son has to learn to accept that – no matter how much he may at first be upset by his Mum being in pain. Research shows that attitudes like this occur again and again in households where violence is common.

Once our society programmes people to behave this way it will remain difficult to change those attitudes without a full understanding of why they are wrong. Those working in this field are making admirable efforts to put the message out in society that attitudes to violence need to be changed. However, it is only with the full understanding that comes from a knowledge of Scripture and a personal knowledge of the heart of God himself that the task will ever fully be achieved.

How should the church respond to domestic violence?

Once the church has accepted that domestic violence is the result of sinful behaviour patterns embedded in our society, the question must be asked – where should the church go from here? The next step should be to look at the effects of the violence in a theological light. Mention has already been made of some of these general effects in chapter 1. These effects themselves are contrary to the type of society God had planned for his creation, which is hardly surprising since evil never breeds good. However, the church needs to look at these effects in the light of Scripture since the result of that study is bound to colour the way in which the church decides to respond to the violence itself. Also, if the church is to address individual instances of family violence, then it needs to know how to deal with the aftermath of the violence.

1. Domestic violence destroys marriages

So often, whether in the church or in families with no religious attachment, violence leads to a divorce. It may take the victim a long time to reach that decision. Research shows that on average a victim suffers around 35 assaults before she seeks assistance. Even then it will usually be a long process before she makes the journey from first admitting she is a victim to being able to make the break from that relationship. Even if she never gets to that stage, be that for economic or emotional reasons or because of her religious principles, the very first incident of violence destroys the spirit of the marriage.

The Bible is clear that marriage is divinely ordained as a good thing. When creating man God said, 'It is not good for the man to be alone. I will make a helper suitable for him' (Gen. 2 :18). This was done before the fall of man. In other words, it was part of God's divine plan that man should be with a woman, a woman who was created out of his own body. Proverbs 18 :22 confirms, 'He who finds a wife finds what is good and receives favour from the LORD.'

Such a marriage is not just about the social union created by a couple committing themselves to each other. It is more than the physical union which results from the act of sexual intercourse. It is also about emotional closeness. It is about mutual trust and confidence, a unique sharing of lives, hopes and aspirations which makes the spouse more important than one's own self.

The marriage ceremony in the Church of England prayer book retains the word 'troth'. According to the *Dictionary of Christian Ethics and Pastoral Theology*, 'Troth is an old English word for fidelity, trust, love and commitment.

Marriage is the ultimate human connection in which two people commit themselves fully and trothfully to each other in a lifelong journey of deep sharing, mutual respect and growing intimacy . . .'

'Therefore', says Genesis 2 :24, 'a man leaves his father and his mother and cleaves to his wife, and they become one flesh' (RSV). 'To "cleave" is an old English word for keeping the troth, clinging to, holding fast. Keeping the troth is counting on each other, giving the utmost, sharing deeply from inside, sticking together through thick and thin.'[2]

This cleaving is mirrored in the Jewish teaching on marriage which, of course, originates from the same Scripture. Jesus came to fulfil the Jewish teaching and not to destroy it, and thus the Old Testament, and godly interpretation of it, is still relevant. Jewish teachers say that the manner of the creation of men and women not only makes marriage the natural state of man but defines the proper relationship within marriage. It is said that the attitude of partners to one another should be one of *'hesed'*. *Hesed* is a word used to describe God, for example in Exodus 34 :6 where the word is qualified by the word *'rav'* or great: 'the LORD, the LORD, the compassionate and gracious God, slow to anger, abounding in love and faithfulness . . . .' *Hesed* is defined as

> 'An ability to give to another out of a sense of closeness and identification with other's needs. One who gives out of *hesed* does so because the other's need is as real to him as his own . . . . *Hesed* is more than the formal dispensation of charity. It includes the ability to shift the entire focus of one's concern . . . acting out of concern for the other's welfare . . . . Marriage is the beginning of *hesed*.'[3]

Domestic violence destroys the marriage troth and is entirely incompatible with *hesed* existing in a relationship. Domestic violence leads to estrangement within the

---

[2] Atkinson, David J. and Field, David H. (eds) *New Dictionary of Pastoral Ethics and Christian Theology* (Leicester: IVP, 1995)
[3] Meiselmann, Moshe, *Jewish Women in Jewish Law* (New York: Yeshiva University Press 1978)

marriage. The parties are no longer united side by side. One is exerting power and control over the other. Trust is replaced by fear. The victim will fear repeated attacks. The abuser may well fear that his victim will leave him, or that she is doing something which he sees as incompatible with her role as partner to him. Sharing is replaced by solitude as the victim retreats from the abuser in an attempt to preserve her dignity and emotional well-being. Caring is replaced by manipulation and domination of the victim by the abuser. The victim can no longer view her husband as her primary source of comfort and protection; if she is to turn for help it will be outside the marriage. If she does not seek help she will be forced to take a stance in opposition to her husband for her self-protection and the safety of the children. The parties will no longer be working together from the inside against outside threats to their relationship. The threat will be within, pitting spouse against spouse.

Mutual recognition of the parties' respective worth and attractiveness is replaced by despising. The victim will now see in the man she married a threat and a danger. Whilst she may very well retain her original love for him, that love will be accompanied by an intense dislike for him because of the violence, whether that dislike is immediately recognized by the woman or not. The husband will begin to see his wife not as someone worthy in her own right but as a wayward partner to be controlled and moulded to his expectation, or as someone on whom he can take out frustrations and anger without a thought for the effect it will have on her. The act of sexual intercourse, which is the physical consummation of the emotional bond, will frequently either be abandoned or in itself turned into a violent act of domination and degradation.

The result is not just the loss of a pleasant social commodity, previously available to both the spouses, but a destruction of the relationship planned and desired by God to bring fulfilment to both parties. John 10:10 reads, 'The thief comes only to steal and kill and destroy; I have come that they may have life, and have it to the full.'

2. Domestic violence destroys the safe environment for children

The Bible presents the ideal picture of children being brought up in a safe and protected environment with clear teaching on what is wrong and right and parental guidance ensuring this teaching is put into practice. Parents are to follow the pattern of God loving his people as a father loves his children. However, the existence of domestic violence destroys any hope of such a safe environment existing. We have already seen in chapter 2 how domestic violence can affect children. These effects are incompatible with biblical teaching on family life.

3. Domestic violence destroys a fullness of life

Jesus stated that he came to give mankind life to the full. The Bible presents a gospel which makes available to all who will accept Christ a life of peace, joy and love. It offers these qualities together with a confidence in others and an honesty and caring when dealing with others. Clearly, in families who do not already have a Christian walk with God, these qualities of life will not already be known in fullness and the violence will exacerbate the effect of living outside of the shelter of God the Father. However, when violence occurs in a marriage where one or both parties know God, the effect is to remove the fullness of life which should exist in that marriage. No man can take away from a Christian the love, peace and joy that comes from the relationship between God and an individual. However, in a Christian relationship those qualities should also be mirrored between individuals as each seeks to enhance the other's Christian walk.

Violence between two parties will damage their relationship. Obviously, this is closely linked with the breaking of troth – and indeed is perhaps best expressed as the practical effects of that break. The victim's life will probably become restricted. She may be forced to remain in the house or to drop certain activities as a result of emotional abuse. Her relationships with family and friends may well be affected. An abuser who is attempting to control his spouse often will prevent her from communication with friends or relations without his express permission. Even when she is free to go where she pleases, or speak to whom she likes, fear, resulting from the abuse, may cause her to voluntarily restrict her actions. If she has visible bruises she may not wish to be seen in public. She may not feel able to talk with full honesty to others because of her own shame. Although her abuser has not expressly forbidden contact with others she may break it off herself in an attempt to stop the violence.

A side effect of the violence will be to destroy the victim's self-confidence. It will become increasingly hard for her to see herself as a person of worth, someone for whom God has planned good things. She may feel abandoned by God in this abusive relationship. Since physical violence is usually accompanied by verbal abuse, a victim who is constantly criticized and told she is no good will have difficulty seizing all life's opportunities with confidence.

The abuser, too, will lose an element of fullness of life. With his own hands and tongue he will be destroying the very relationship which God created for his good. If the violence is known or suspected he may be shunned by former friends and his church activities may be restricted. His relationship with his children will be damaged and he may even find himself having to face legal proceedings with their attendant social and financial consequences. His sin will be preventing him having a full walk with God:

> If we claim to have fellowship with him yet walk in the darkness, we lie and do not live by the truth. But if we walk in the light, as he is in the light, we have fellowship with one another, and the blood of Jesus, his Son, purifies us from every sin (1 Jn. 1 :6).

4. Domestic violence causes knock-on side effects

Violence in the family is a form of oppression which is also condemned in the Bible. It may drive the woman to have to take the children and leave the home. This departure often causes poverty. In all cases of divorce, the effect of separation is that the parties both suffer a drop in living standards as one pot of money has to support two families. However, in cases of domestic violence, victims and children are often forced to leave as a matter of urgency, often ending up in refuge accommodation. Wives are forced to become dependant on welfare benefits – if not in the long term, then at least until the finances are sorted out by a lawyer. Children often effectively lose their fathers; a mother may still allow contact with the father depending on her assessment of risk to the children. However, in some cases of more severe abuse, the assessment will be that the children are in danger if left alone with their own father. In those circumstances, contact may be arranged for short times with a third party to ensure the child's protection – so called 'supervised contact'. However, the presence of the third party obviously restricts the father-child relationship. In extreme cases, a victim may need to simply leave the area without trace to escape from the violence. In those circumstances children may lose their father completely.

Poverty, oppression and fatherless children are all things which grieve the father heart of God. He is not prepared to stand by and see these people suffer. Psalm 72 :12-14 reads:

> For he will deliver the needy who cry out, the afflicted who have no-one to help. He will take pity on the weak and the needy and save the needy from death. He will rescue them from oppression and violence, for precious is their blood in his sight (see also Ps. 35 :10).

As God's people on earth, the church must adopt his attitude to these victims.

The 'public / private dichotomy'

The question then becomes, what should the church's response to the issue of domestic violence be? Secular responses have depended on which side of the so-called 'public / private dichotomy' the individual or body concerned has taken. The phrase 'public / private dichotomy' expresses the view that responses to social problems depend on whether a problem is classified as a public or private one. For example, the phrase has been used in analysis of why the police traditionally have been reluctant to respond to incidents of domestic violence. It is argued that the police believed they should concentrate on public order policing and, as a consequence, they have marginalized private or domestic crime. Thus, issues such as public demonstrations, street muggings or drug trafficking have occupied police time at the expense of crimes which occurred behind closed doors. This was because such 'street crime' was seen as being against society as a whole. Society, being a corporate identity rather than an individual one, could not respond for itself and therefore it was the role of the police to act as the custodians of that society's well-being. On the other hand, the so-called 'domestic crime' happened between adult victims who were seen as being responsible for taking their own actions by using the civil law. In other words, the argument was that crime against the public should be dealt with in the public arena, while crimes against individuals were a private matter to be dealt with accordingly.

As the result of efforts made by those working in domestic violence, this attitude is changing. The police are now far more aware of their role in reacting to incidents of domestic violence. Other social bodies such as the courts and social services are also becoming more involved. However, the church faces the same dilemma. How should it best respond to domestic violence whilst seeking to uphold family values? These same two options of public and private response are open to the church.

1. 'A private response'

This view sees domestic violence as the woman's private struggle in the context of her relationship with the abuser and of her own spiritual life. It argues that domestic violence should be dealt with in that private, personal and sacred relationship between man and wife, and outsiders should not interfere in that relationship. The violence is seen as a problem between those individuals alone, rather than a social problem. It is termed a 'trial and tribulation' which the woman must live through as part of her Christian walk. She might be told to pray harder and try to be a better wife so that her husband might be changed by her attitude. In other words, this response places the blame solely on the individual – either victim or abuser or both.

Such a view is often tied up with scriptural teaching on submission. At its most extreme, the reaction is that because the woman is subject to the man he has the right to beat her. Even if it does not go that far, a 'private response' characteristically states that because the woman is subject to the man she has to put up with it alone. It is her cross to bear in submission, and the man's authority over his wife means that it is inappropriate for anyone else to intervene, since that would disturb that chain of authority. The wife should be left to her marriage – for better or for worse.

2. 'A public response'

It is argued throughout this book that it is correct to take a much more 'public response'. Domestic violence should be acknowledged as a problem which is embedded in the very fabric of our society. We have already seen how this occurs in the spiritual realm, and chapter 4 will show how it is achieved in the social realm. While recognizing that the problem is a social one, it is still necessary to place it in the context of the individual's sin and responsibility. There should be a public condemnation of and reaction to the sin and a public, practical response to the issue. The church needs to be heard to condemn domestic violence in its pulpits and in its Bible studies and marriage preparation classes. Its voice also needs to be heard by those outside the church walls. The church needs as well to become active in caring practically for victims of domestic violence. It needs to actively promote social reforms and programmes which help to deal with the problem.

What about submission?

In order to take the 'public response' view it is necessary to examine the scriptural teachings on submission. It is perhaps this teaching more than any other which causes people to be reluctant about becoming fully involved in fighting domestic violence. In particular, the problematic passage is often Ephesians 5 :21-33:

> Submit to one another out of reverence for Christ.
>
> Wives, submit to your husbands as to the Lord. For the husband is the head of the wife as Christ is the head of the church, his body, of which he is the Saviour. Now as the church submits to Christ, so also wives should submit to their husbands in everything.
>
> Husbands, love your wives, just as Christ loved the church and gave himself up for her to make her holy, cleansing her by the washing with water through the word, and to present her to himself as a radiant church, without stain or wrinkle or any other blemish, but holy and blameless. In this same way, husbands ought to love their wives as their own bodies. He who loves his wife loves himself. After all, no-one ever hated his own body, but he feeds and cares for it, just as Christ does the church – for we are members of his body. "For this reason a man will leave his father and mother and be united to his wife, and the two will become one flesh." This is a profound mystery – but I am talking about Christ and the church. However, each one of you also must love his wife as he loves himself, and the wife must respect her husband.

Biblical teaching on submission is in fact rooted in teaching on love. It is also intertwined with the relationship between the church and Christ as its head. So, the first step is to look at the concept of the submission of the church to Christ.

The church comes to Christ with trust and love because of his care for the church and the individuals who make up that church. Christ cherishes, loves and protects his people. The picture of God sheltering his people under the shadow of his wings is a powerful one (Ps. 17 :8; Mt 23 :37). Likewise, the concept of God covering his people with the shadow of his hand, the same hand that created the world, creates an image of extreme power used not in anger but to shelter, protect and show tenderness (see Is. 51 :16; Ex. 33 :22). The church comes to Christ with full confidence that he will not harm them. Christ is head of the church. However, despite his power and authority, he does not reign as a despot, imposing his will. Rather he is a servant king, giving free will, choice, benefit and fulfilment to his bride.

The Bible shows that the human marriage is a reflection of the relationship between God and his church. Therefore, the teaching on submission between the church and Christ is equally applicable to husband and wife. Submission in marriage is presented as a two-way process of responsibility.

1. 'Wives submit as to the Lord'

In other words, the wife is to place the same trust and confidence in her husband as she does in her Lord. So submission is not a command to allow oneself to be subjected to degradation but is rather an exhortation to live in faith. Trust and confidence in the husband is a prerequisite without which the wife cannot open herself up to the intimate union intended to exist in marriage. The teaching on submission is an exhortation not to remain aloof and independent and so miss out on the benefits and fulfilment to be found in marriage. There is an element of vulnerability in this submission but it should be a case of giving to gain.

2. 'Husbands, love your wives, just as Christ loves the church'

Husbands have a mirror role to play. They need to love, just as Christ loved the church. This love is about self-sacrifice and always acting in her best interests – in itself a form of submission expressed in different words. Indeed verse 21 states that all Christians should submit to one another. This teaching does not allow for the causing of pain, for violence or rejection. Instead, the pictures of God returning to a faithless wife should be borne in mind. Husbands are to love their wives as they do their own bodies. It is generally accepted that causing pain to oneself or using violence against one's own body is a sign of mental illness and is not normal behaviour.

This attitude of mutual submission is expressed in verse 33. The wife is told to respect her husband. The danger in modern society is to see someone who is self-sacrificing as a 'wimp' – someone open to exploitation. In fact, wives should recognise the burden of the responsibility to love as selflessly and completely as Christ loved.

Two other brief points can be made as an adjunct to this interpretation. Firstly, any authority which is given to man is given by God. Violence in a relationship exceeds this authority and cannot, therefore, be godly. Secondly, there is no biblical authority given to use violence to obtain the submission of the other spouse.

Indeed, the Bible specifically condemns violence in the context of marriage. Malachi 2 :16 reads, 'I hate divorce, says the LORD the God of Israel, and covering one's garment with violence, says the LORD of Hosts.' (RSV) This condemnation of violence refers specifically to marriage relationships. Its significance lies in the symbolism of the garment in the context of marriage. The casting of a garment over a woman was symbolic of him claiming her as a wife – see for example Ruth 3 :9, when Ruth said to Boaz, "'I am your servant Ruth. Spread the corner of your garment over me, since you are a kinsman-redeemer.'"

Ezekiel employs the same phrase when using marriage imagery to describe God's relationship with his people (Ez 16 :8), 'Later I passed by, and when I looked at you and saw that you were old enough for love, I spread the corner of my garment over you and covered your nakedness.' The garment was symbolic of the provision and protection the man would give his bride in the future. In the verse in Malachi, God is specifically stating that he hates it when a covering of violence is placed on top of the marriage relationship. The above reading is to be preferred, being used in the RSV, NIV, NASB, and Darby translations. It is interesting, however, that the KJV places the words the other way around, reading, 'For the LORD, the God of Israel, saith that he hateth putting away: for one covereth violence with his garment, saith the LORD of hosts.' Similarly, the YLT version reads, 'For I hate sending away, said Jehovah, God of Israel,I and He who hath covered violence with his clothing.' Even from these readings it can be seen that it is not acceptable to God that violence be hidden behind a screen of marriage. Such violence should not be termed a 'private matter' and hidden behind closed doors.

Eradication or escape?

If the church takes this public stance against domestic violence, it is faced with a seemingly contradictory two-fold duty. Firstly, it needs to protect the oppressed and needy. However, this protection may involve intervention which, on the face of it, threatens the second duty – to uphold the family unit.

The traditional societal response to domestic violence has been to facilitate the victim's *escape* from the violence. How and why this has been done will be examined in chapter 6. However, let it suffice to say here that the effect of this response has been to take the victim out of the violence by destroying or threatening the family unit while leaving the abuser's violent tendencies unaddressed. Victims are encouraged to leave for a refuge or take out an injunction through the courts to prevent the abuser coming to the matrimonial home. Since these are temporary measures, they are usually followed by a divorce or permanent separation. The abuser is just left, and no attention is given to the original cause of the violence. Thus, the problem is not solved – the violence has not been stopped. The way has just been made open for the victim to suffer the attendant problems inherent in the breakdown of a marriage. Further, no steps have been taken to ensure that a second victim does not take her place.

This book argues throughout that a more appropriate response is to focus on the eradication of the problem. That is to say, we should focus on ensuring that the violence stops altogether. That may well mean a temporary splitting of the family unit for the victim's protection. However, the long-term aim should be to keep that family together but without the violence. This idea is developed further in chapter 8.

Again, before moving further with this concept of eradication of violence it is important that its theological basis be established. We have already seen that the Bible's emphasis is on marriage and that God hates divorce. However, there are other biblical grounds for focusing on eradicating the problem rather than just facilitating a victim's escape from it.

1. Healing and recreation

The Bible, indeed the whole gospel message itself, emphasizes healing and the recreation of something good out of destruction. The Old Testament frequently uses imagery which talks of barren and desolate places being made beautiful again. It is not suggested that another, better place is found and the old abandoned, but that with a godly touch good comes out of the old. For example, in Isaiah 35 :1-2,6-7,

> The desert and the parched land will be glad; the wilderness will rejoice and blossom. Like the crocus, it will burst into bloom; it will rejoice greatly and shout for joy... Water will gush forth in the wilderness and streams in the desert. The burning sand will become a pool, the thirsty ground bubbling springs. In the haunts where jackals once lay, grass and reeds and papyrus will grow.

Escaping from the violence by divorce or separation only adds to the pain of the victim and her children. Most victims do not really want to leave; they just want the violence to stop. It is the seeming impossibility of that which forces such women to leave their abusers. Fortunately, the good news of the Bible is that, 'Nothing is impossible with God' (Lk 1 :37).

2. High places

The wife's escape from the violence leaves the husband's violent tendencies untreated. Many abusers who experience a broken relationship go on to enter into further relationships in which the pattern of violence repeats itself. The Bible teaches that sin should be destroyed, not merely set aside. An example is the Bible's attitude to the so-called 'high places', the places used for idol worship by the heathen nations when Israel entered the promised land. Since Israel had no need for these shrines, they could have simply been left to rot and decay in the elements. Not so. The Israelites were commanded to destroy them completely to ensure that the temptation to use them in idol worship was removed. According to Numbers 33 :51-52, 'When you cross the Jordan into Canaan, drive out all the inhabitants of the land before you. Destroy all their carved images and their cast idols, and demolish all their high places.' (see also Lv. 26 :30; 2 Ch. 14 :2) Following this spiritual principle, the attitude of the church should be to try to destroy all vestiges of tendencies towards domestic violence.

3. Divorce is not sanctioned

There are differing interpretations of Scripture as to whether divorce and remarriage is permitted where there has been adultery. However, it is clear that there is no sanction for divorce because of violence between the spouses. In Mark 10 :1-12, the Pharisees, who were questioning Jesus, were actually testing his reaction to divergent teachings of eminent rabbis. On one hand, some taught that divorce was only permitted in cases of adultery. Other rabbis were much more liberal and allowed divorce in a whole range of circumstances. Jesus' condemnation of this second view was clear: 'What God has joined together, let man not separate.'

However, violence is incompatible with the biblical pattern of marriage. To let violence continue would be unjust. Justice cannot operate when God's laws and principles are being broken. Habakkuk recognised this when he cried out to God, 'Destruction and violence are before me; there is strife, and conflict abounds. Therefore the law is paralysed, and justice never prevails' (1 :3-4). It is almost as if God's laws and principles act as a belt holding up the trousers of justice. If those principles are slackened, justice falls (see Jer. 13 :1-11).

The church should be concerned with preventing injustices and ensuring that those who are subject to injustice are fully recompensed. This does not mean merely stopping the unjust action and placing the victim in a position of neutrality. It means restoring to victims all the benefits they would have had if justice had prevailed. As God said in Joel 2 :25, 'I will repay you for the years the locusts have eaten.' In dealing with domestic violence, the church should be concerned with not only stopping the violence, but also with rebuilding those damaged relationships.

4. *The father heart of God*

The church needs to react to domestic violence with the father heart of God. God does not just condemn those things which displease him. He is shown in the Bible to be a God who takes action to save and rescue his people from those things which threaten to harm or destroy them. If the church is to effectively operate as God's body on earth, then it needs to feel the same pain Habakkuk did when surveying the state his society was in. Habakkuk cried out continually to God, and despite what seemed an impossible situation he refused to give up until God had revealed to him how the injustices rampant in his society were to be vanquished:

> How long, O LORD must I call for help, but you do not listen? Or cry out to you, 'violence!' but you do not save? Why do you make me look at injustice? Why do you tolerate wrong?....Why are you silent while the wicked swallow up those more righteous than themselves?...I will stand at my watch and station myself on the ramparts; I will look to see what he will say to me, and what answer I am to give to this complaint (Hab. 1 :2-3,13; 2 :1).

Tackling the issue of domestic violence is never going to

be easy or quick. It is a pernicious social phenomenon which has taken root in our society and which can only ever be fully defeated by bringing the gospel truth into those situations where it has taken hold. Admirable efforts are being taken by a whole range of social bodies to combat the problem, as will be discussed later. However, since it is only the healing which comes from reconciliation with Christ himself which can truly end all the hurt and pain caused by domestic violence, it is vital that the church joins with these agencies to combat the problem. If it is accepted that domestic violence has its roots in the spiritual realm, then it must follow that only the church has the power and authority to fight against that violence in the spiritual realm. Only the church has full access to the weapons needed for that warfare: the belt of truth, the breastplate of righteousness, the readiness which comes from the gospel of Christ, the shield of faith, the helmet of salvation and the sword of the Spirit (Eph. 6 :13ff). It is the church's responsibility to take spiritual and practical measures to bring about the eradication of domestic violence and to offer healing to its victims.

Four

A Causation Model – Combining the Theories

What causes domestic violence? What motivates those who abuse their partners? Is it their conscious choice or is it inherent in their upbringing or personality? Why does it affect some families but not others? Is it all down to the individuals involved or does the responsibility lie with society as a whole? Is it an 'inherited' tendency or is the problem one which strikes on an entirely random basis?

Anyone wanting to help victims of domestic violence will need to ask these kinds of questions, since the answers will inevitably influence the way they choose to deal with the problem. Let us use the analogy of a tree with diseased leaves. A gardener could disregard how the leaves got to be full of holes or to have nasty white patches all over them; he could just pull the leaves off. However, that would leave the tree bare and would not stop new leaves from being similarly diseased. If he is to really deal with the problem, then he will want to consider a more effective treatment. The form of that treatment will depend on the cause. If the cause is a disease in the root of the tree he may want to put chemicals down into the soil. If the problem is that a particular insect is eating the leaves he may want to spray the leaves with something unpleasant to that insect.

In a sense, it is the same with social problems. If intervention into a family is to be on anything more than a superficial basis, those offering assistance must try to deal with the underlying causes as well as the symptoms. It is only in relatively recent times that research programmes have looked into the causes of family violence. However, in those 30 or so years, various researchers have come up with a number of theories.

The first research tended to take a psychiatric approach. Domestic violence was seen as being linked to individual characteristics of the abuser. The violence was put down to personality defects, psychopathy or substance misuse which produced an aggressive reaction. In other words, there was something wrong with the abuser which distinguished him from other 'normal' men. To some extent, this can be comforting. Not only does it make domestic violence seem less likely to occur in families close to us, but it also absolves the observer of the violence from any responsibility.

Later studies, however, discredited such assumptions. Research was done in 1978 which found that less than ten per cent of incidents of domestic violence are attributable to factors such as those listed above. So later research had to look in a different direction. More recent explanations now tend to focus more on aspects of society or features of a family's situation which might cause or exacerbate violence.

Despite all this research there has not, to date, been one theory or explanation which in itself can give a satisfactory answer. Any given explanation could be true for one family but not another. Taken together, however, these explanations offer a much clearer picture. It is as if each theory is like one type of building material. Alone, a pile of bricks will fall down. Alone, a window will not provide a home. If all the materials are put together in the right way, however, bricks, mortar, tiles, glass, etc., will make a house. Similarly, if the theories are combined, the complete picture emerges. This chapter will show how these theories can be put together, and the diagrams help to give a visual picture of the combination.

On top of this 'combined model of causation' should be added another layer: the Christian perspective. Chapter 3 looked at the biblical teaching relevant to domestic violence. Church members will want to bear that teaching in mind when considering the sociological theories mentioned in this chapter. This exercise reveals how sin has manifested itself like a liana plant in our society. Sin has taken root in various aspects of our culture and has spread, creating the tangled web which is domestic violence today.

The cultural patterning of violence

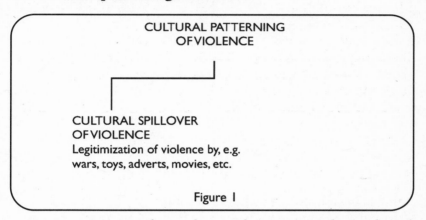

CULTURAL PATTERNING
OF VIOLENCE

CULTURAL SPILLOVER
OF VIOLENCE
Legitimization of violence by, e.g.
wars, toys, adverts, movies, etc.

Figure I

Let us start with a theory known as the cultural patterning of violence. This theory, in essence, says that violence is part of our culture, part of the normal day-to-day life in our society. It is, therefore, not surprising that violence should take place in some of our families, since families are part of our culture too. In other words, just as Christmas celebrations are part of our culture and families develop their own Christmas traditions, so violence is a part of our culture and families become involved in violence too. This concept of violence as a cultural problem is a convenient starting point but can then be broken down a little further. Also, theories which are presented as answers on their own can be brought in as strands of this larger argument.

As Figure 2 shows, there are two main strands to this theory that violence is a cultural problem – the cultural spillover of violence and cultural consistency.

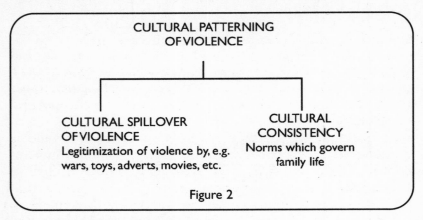

Figure 2

1. Cultural spillover of violence

The first point is that violence spills over from other spheres of life into the family arena. A useful comparison is the spreading of the plague into medieval country villages. Imagine the family unit to be like an isolated country village. It is as much a part of Britain, of society, as the port which lies, say, 30 miles to the south. However, the villagers tend to be self-contained and to all intents and purposes for them the plague which enters Britain through that port may as well be a disease affecting only the moon. Until, that is, travelling salesmen begin to visit the village market to sell their wares. As these tradesmen come into the village they bring with them things from outside the village: pegs, perhaps, horses and, unfortunately, the deadly plague. The only way to protect the village is for it to maintain complete isolation. To some extent, family units are the same. No matter how tight and inward-looking they are, they cannot help but be influenced by what is going on in the society around them.

This cultural spillover theory, therefore, says that violence in the family is a reflection of the fact that violence is common in other areas of our life. Baron and Straus wrote:

> The more a society tends to endorse the use of physical force to attain socially approved ends (such as order in the schools, crime control and international dominance) the greater is the likelihood that this legitimisation of force will be generalised to other spheres of life where force is less socially approved such as the family and the relations between the sexes.[1]

In other words, it is suggested that domestic violence is a pattern of behaviour which is derived from the perpetrator being constantly immersed in a culture which accepts and promotes violence.

It is not hard to think of ways in which violence is stimulated and encouraged in our society. Violent films are commonplace. Following the murder of Jamie Bulger in Liverpool by two young boys, there was some concern that the crime was similar to one depicted in a violent video which these children had been allowed to watch. So called 'snuff' movies specifically depict women as victims of violence. However even mainstream films, fit for viewing by teenagers, offer violence as a form of entertainment.

Another example is the sanctioning of violence in war. Whilst defence of a state will be, in most incidences of war, a justifiable measure, it is still violence which is sanctioned by the state as an acceptable means to an end. Increasingly, war is taking on entertainment status as well. It is a long way from the lonely horrors of the First World War poppy fields to the Gulf War during which we were able to sit in our homes and be entertained by live coverage of Smart bombs attacking Baghdad. Gurr did an interesting study on this and found that, following a continual decline in the murder and non-negligent manslaughter rate in the United States since the nineteen-thirties, the rates for these crimes more than doubled during the Vietnam War.[2]

---

[1] Baron, L. and Straus, M.A., 'Legitimate violence and rape: A test of the cultural spill-over theory, (Durham, Family Research Laboratory, University of New Hampshire 1983, Unpublished)

[2] Gurr in Goldstein, J.H., *Aggression and Crimes of Violence* (Oxford: Oxford University Press 1986)

Sometimes advertisements portray women as victims of violence. Adverts are specifically designed to sell the idea behind them, so they can have a powerful effect when beamed into the home on our television or reproduced in magazines. The formation of the organization Women Against Violence Against Women was inspired by a hoarding in Los Angeles some years ago which advertised the Rolling Stones' album, 'Black and Blue'. The advert showed a woman in tattered clothes with her hands chained. Her facial expression was one of sexual excitement whilst the caption read 'She loves it!'

At other times violence can be packaged as humour. One Finnair advert once read, 'How Vilho Vatanen the Finn created the world's first sauna when he locked his wife in the smokehouse, set it on fire, beat her soundly with birch leaves and discovered that she loved it.' Every summer, crowds gather around seaside Punch and Judy stalls and laugh as Punch beats Judy about the head. We can probably all think of at least one film recently in which humour has been combined with some violence incident. Indeed, it is often the stuff of which the best films are made. So, is there any harm in it? According to research done by Ellis and Sekyra, there may well be – their results found that, rather than aggressive humour having a cathartic effect, it can actually stimulate aggressive behaviour.[3]

Violence is also packaged as recreation. Children's toys often take the form of replicas of imaginary weapons, whilst video games revolve around destruction of 'the enemy'. Sports such as boxing and wrestling are overtly violent whilst others incorporate acts of aggression as part of the general ethos of the game. Again, the spillover effect has been documented in research which shows a high correlation between the amount of violence on the playing field and the amount of violence in the stands. Phillips showed that a short-run spurt in homicide followed each heavyweight boxing championship in the USA between

[3] Ellis, G.T. and Sekyra, F., 'The effect of aggressive cartoons on the behaviour of first grade children' *Journal of Psychology* 81 (1972) pp.37-43

1973 and 1978. Of course it is always hard, if not impossible, to prove that such a correlation also indicated a causal effect. Nevertheless, the idea of violence in sport encouraging violence in other areas of life is consistent with an explanation by Goldstein of the social function of team games. He wrote,

> Games and sport serve a variety of functions – from teaching young participants to abide by formally prescribed rules of conduct to the fostering of competition between teams and co-operation between teams. Both participants and spectators may learn abstract principles for behaviour from the rules of games.[4]

Thus the games which are popularly used in schools to foster team spirit and unselfishness may in fact be fostering violent and aggressive conduct.

Perhaps the most common and far-reaching examples of violence are to be seen on the television. Even children's cartoons these days are violent, be it Teenage Mutant Ninja Turtles or Power Rangers. Dramas feature shootings, murders and rapes. The soap operas have fights and brawls from time to time. In 1995 a survey was carried out by academics at Sheffield University, commissioned by the BBC and the Independent Television Commission, on the levels of violence on our TV screens. They found that in terms of overall time, the level of violence was low. It has, in fact, declined from 1.1 per cent of screen time in 1986 to 0.61 per cent in 1994–95. However, there was still a very regular occurrence of violent incidents. The study monitored 4,715 hours of programmes and observed no less than twenty-one thousand separate violent acts in ten thousand violent sequences. Violence was defined as 'the intention to harm or intimidate'. Interestingly, much of the violence was in feature films, but the children's programme *Teenage Mutant Ninja Turtles* contained no less than 142 acts of violence. In the four-week sample the percentages of programmes on each channel surveyed which contained violence were:

---

4 Goldstein, G.H., *Sports Violence* (1983) p.51

- BBC1 - 27%

- BBC2 - 23%

- ITV - 29%

- Channel 4 - 30%

- Sky 1 - 37%

- UK Gold - 38%

- Sky Movies - 79%

- Movie Channel - 81%[5]

There are two conflicting theories as to the effect of screen violence. The first, the 'catharsis theory,' claims that the inherently aggressive impulses which every human being has may be satisfied by identifying with others whom they see acting violently. So, it is argued, on a day when you want to throttle your boss or slap a particularly bolshy child, these desires can be satisfied by proxy, as it were, by watching a film character take a good beating at the hands of Sylvester Stallone.

However, evidence from research is available to refute this with one study finding *increased* aggressiveness in college students after they saw physical assaults on film. Negative effects of violent television can be divided into short-term 'cueing' or 'triggering' effects, whereby screen portrayal of violence directly inspires a violent act by the viewer, and longer-term effects. 'Desensitization theory' says that the long term effects of violence on television include an indifference to aggression and thus more tolerance of its occurrence. In other words, it gradually loses its shock value and becomes more commonplace and expected. One report also found that exposure to screen violence can lead to an exaggerated sense of danger and mistrust, creating fearfulness and difficulty in distinguishing between fact and fantasy. This confusion

---

[5] Department of Journalism Studies, Sheffield University. Quoted in *Television and Censorship* Donnellan, C. (ed) (Cambridge: Independence 1996)

may be particularly significant in the context of domestic violence, since many incidents of domestic violence are linked with accusations of unfaithfulness which are untrue.

In fact, research on this topic continues, and, it is generally agreed by those within the entertainment industry, there is no definite proof that violence on screen leads to violence in real life. However, neither can it be definitively proved that it does not. Interesting comments were made in an article written by Melvin Bragg in the *Independent* newspaper in August 1995 and in letters responding to the article.

Melvin Bragg was writing about a book called *Moving Experiences: Understanding Television's Influences and Effects* by David Gauntlett which, Bragg says:

> has ranged over the mountains of research into TV, a great deal of it tenaciously determined to prove the box to be the villain. In effect, this case does not add up to a row of beans. Of course, TV has an influence. Like newspapers, movies, novels, parents, peers, heroes, work, non-work, genes and so on. No one denies that. What Gauntlett does deny, authoritatively, is the repeated assertion that – to take the hottest area – acts of violence on the TV cause acts of violence in society. The most careful sifting of decades of research shows this to be mistaken.[6]

In response to this article, J.M. Wober, a principle lecturer at the Department of Media Production, Poole, Dorset wrote to the editor saying, *inter alia:*

> . . . [the book by David Gauntlett] does not contain any new information but consists of quite familiar sociological criticisms of various original studies that have mostly been carried out by psychologists . . . . [it] misjudges many studies and omits others that are important . . . The true interpretation is surely, that screen violence has a small effect on some people, in interaction with other influences. We can, however, reasonably readily reduce the amount of screen violence, and it is probably healthy to do so.[7]

---

[6] Bragg, M., 'You can't blame it on the box', in Donnellan, C. (ed) *Violence in the Family* (Cambridge: Independence 1995) p.4

[7] Wober, J.M., in Donnellan, C. (ed) *Violence in the Family* (Cambridge: Independence 1995) p.5

Philip Graham, Chair of the National Children's Bureau, also wrote, saying:

> . . . there is a strong consensus, reflected in several recent academic reviews, that the scientific evidence supports the view that violent media images play a small but definite part in raising the level of violence in our society, particularly among vulnerable groups, but that there are more important, adverse influences.[8]

The interesting thing about this debate is that, whatever one thinks about the research, all seem to agree that screen violence is an influence on people's behaviour even if it is not a direct cause of violence. This fits in well with the argument that cultural values combine to produce a culture in which violence sits comfortably.

The media through which violence in society is encouraged and stimulated – television, games, films and so on – are not wrong in themselves. All these are tools which have potential for good or bad, depending on the context in which they are used. Indeed, there is now a growing market in Christian television programmes and even board games. These forms of communication are neutral but can be channels for the attitudes of those using them.

Philippians 4 :8 makes clear the standards expected of Christians in circumstances in which they have a discretion as to how to act: 'Finally, brothers, whatever is true, whatever is noble, whatever is right, whatever is pure, whatever is lovely, whatever is admirable – if anything is excellent or praiseworthy – think about such things.' Chapter 3 has already looked at the biblical teaching on violence in general which makes it clear that recreational violence, whatever current society says, is far from admirable, noble or right. The prevalence of media violence is, therefore, a form of sin which has become part of our society's structure. A number of the words used for sin, referred to in chapter 3, apply. Media violence 'misses the mark' (*chattah*) in the sense that it does not reach the

---

[8] Graham, P., in Donnellan, C. (ed) *Violence in the Family* (Cambridge: Independence 1995) p.5

standard of purity set down in Scripture. It is also swerving over the boundaries (*parabasis*) set by such verses as that quoted above. It errs (*shagah*) as well in the misuse of neutral commodities which could be used for good.

2. The cultural consistency theory

The second strand to the argument that domestic violence comes out of our culture is the so-called 'cultural consistency theory'. This theory says that our culture incorporates certain values. These values are not really concerned with violence in themselves, but they do govern family life. They do so in a way which can both lead to and perpetuate violence within a family. In other words, violence in the family fits in with, and is not alien to, other cultural values affecting the family.

Let us take another example to illustrate the point. Some orthodox Jewish groups hold cultural values which say that images of humans are forbidden. This idea is based entirely on their interpretation of the biblical command prohibiting graven images. It has nothing to do with modern technology and is something which has been passed down for generations, well before the age of computers. However, when the Internet became popular, a problem was created. If these Jews were to 'surf the net', looking through pages of electronic information and pictures entirely at random, then they might inadvertently sin by coming across such a picture. So, a decision was made to have censors. Now, the values here are not directly to do with censorship; they are religious values which go much deeper. However, they are values which make censorship possible and acceptable.

The cultural consistency theory says that, in the same way, we hold values in our society which make domestic violence possible and acceptable. The idea of a link between family life and wider community values is not a new one. Indeed, the Israelites settling in the promised land were forbidden from intermarrying with the nations already in occupation of that land. Deuteronomy 7 :3 refers to the nations they were about to encounter; 'Do not intermarry with them. Do not give your daughters to their sons or take their daughters for your sons, for they will turn your sons away from following me to serve other gods.' The admonition is repeated in Joshua 23 :12-13, when it is stated that intermarriage would make the other nations '. . . snares and traps for you, whips on your backs and thorns in your eyes, until you perish from this good land, which the LORD your God has given you.'

The problem with intermarriage was that the spouse would inevitably bring into the family life the culture, and more particularly the religion, of her own people. One of the benefits of the Jewish food laws and the other laws regulating family activities is that they keep the family focused on the religious principles symbolized by the rituals. Food laws made it difficult for the Israelites to socialize outside the community and so the spillover effect of the foreigners' cultural values was minimized.

Of course, the major purpose of limiting spillover of cultural values in biblical times was to avoid idolatry since it was the exclusive worship of God which made Israel a 'separate people'. Nevertheless, the principle remains that the culture of a society as a whole is inextricably linked to family life.

It is at this stage that the diagram becomes a little more complicated as we begin to draw in some other theories as to the cause of domestic violence. The 'patriarchal theory,' the 'status inconsistency theory' and the 'theory of power differentials' are all theories which have been presented as being reasons for domestic violence. In fact, as we shall see, if left to stand on their own, each is a rather incomplete explanation. However, they fit into a more comprehensive model as examples of the values which are referred to in the cultural consistency theory. Let us examine each one in turn.

a) Patriarchal theory

The patriarchal theory is closely associated with the feminist perspectives on domestic violence. Writers such as the Dobashes, who are heavily involved in domestic violence research, claim that the phenomenon of wife abuse should be regarded not as abnormal or deviant behaviour: 'Rather, it is a form of behaviour which has existed for centuries as an acceptable and, indeed, desirable part of a family system within a patriarchal society.'[9]

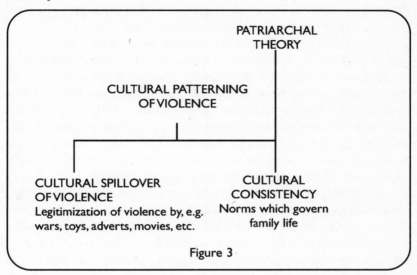

Figure 3

Those who hold to this theory argue that our society is male-dominated and that power is vested in men to dominate and to control women. They also argue that society lets men use whatever means are necessary to retain that authority should a woman dare to challenge them. Some writers stop here. All they say is that it is a man's world, and so domestic violence is not surprising. Others, like Straus and Hotaling, go a little further. They identify nine specific values which are common in our society and which 'create and maintain a high level of marital violence'.[10]

Many of these nine values reflect gender stereotypes which exist in our society. They refer to the 'compulsive

[9] Dobash, R.E. and Dobash, R.P., 'Wives: the "appropriate" victims of domestic violence' *Victimology* 2 (314) (1978) pp.426-42

[10] Straus, M. and Hotaling, G., *The Social Causes of Husband – Wife Violence* (University of Minnesota 1979)

masculinity' and the 'defence of male authority', meaning that if men find that they have lost their superiority in a relationship they will use violence to reclaim it. Other values concern a woman's place in the family compared to a man's. They argue that women are traditionally seen as having a 'wife role' or as being 'childlike', implying that they need chastisement from time to time.

The remaining five values describe other aspects of society which perpetuate family violence. They talk about 'economic constraints and discrimination' which, combined with 'the burden of childcare', coerce women into remaining in violent relationships. If it is hard for women to find well-paid work and difficult for them to find suitable childcare to take up any job which may come along, then women may feel they cannot strike out in a new life alone. The 'negative self-image' which many women develop as a result of the emphasis in society on competitive achievement makes them more vulnerable to accepting violence. On top of all that, 'male orientation of the criminal justice system' makes legal relief difficult to obtain. If those handing out justice believe that there is nothing inherently wrong with a man hitting his wife, then sentences for assault are likely to be light and mitigating factors such as provocation are more likely to be allowed.

Again, looking at these cultural norms from a theological perspective, we can see that they are, in essence, structuralized forms of sin. Biblical teaching on submission and dual, sharing, interdependant roles in marriage have been perverted into inappropriate submission of women. Discrimination, oppression and suppression of justice are all condemned throughout the Bible.

On its own, the patriarchal theory is difficult to verify and does not explain why violence, as opposed to any other means, is used to perpetuate such male dominance. It is practically disproved as a general explanation of all domestic violence if one accepts that men can be victims too. However, it is undoubtedly true that there is general stereotyping of women in society and discrimination against them does still exist. Patriarchism, then, can be seen as a collection of cultural values which govern family life. Violence by men on women is not inconsistent with these values.

b) Status inconsistency theory

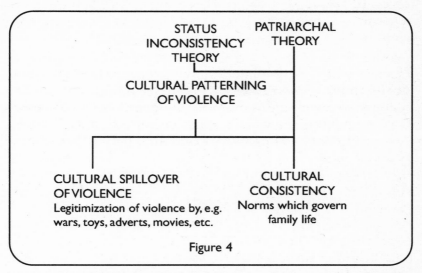

Figure 4

Another theory is that domestic violence is born of the frustration that occurs when the abuser perceives his status within the home as being lower than it should be. This is especially so when the abuser's power has eroded whilst the victim's has increased. Often this power is financial – perhaps the abuser was always the breadwinner but now he is unemployed and has to live off his wife's new part-time earnings. Or perhaps frustration arises because the abuser has a higher education than his job demands – for example, perhaps a bank clerk who was made redundant has to work as a window cleaner.

This theory is based on the idea that frustration, caused by such inconsistencies in status, builds up and is eventually taken out on the victim. However, as a single theory, it does not explain why that frustration is so great, nor why it results in violence rather than any other form of expression. Again, it is more useful to look at the theory as an example of cultural values which tie in with domestic violence. The fact that a man in this position would find himself frustrated presupposes that he holds values, for example, that the man should be the breadwinner or that he should be the leader in the relationship. When those values are threatened he looks around for a way to re-establish them. If it is not possible for him to earn more money or get a better job, then, according to the cultural spillover theory, violence will not be an unacceptable way for him to regain control.

c) The theory of power differentials

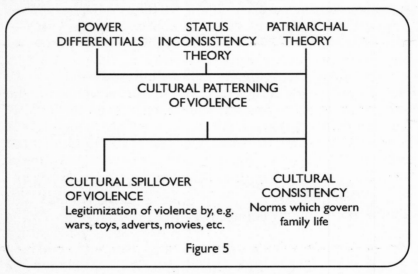

Figure 5

Power is a very important factor in domestic violence. Finkelhor notes:

> The most common patterns are not just for the more powerful to abuse the less powerful, but for the most powerful to abuse the least. This is an interesting commonality. Abuse tends to gravitate to the relationship of greatest power differential.[11]

This often is the case when the abuser is low on power outside the home but can create, or keep, great power in the home by his use of violence. The home may be the only

---

[11] Finkelhor, D., Gelles, R.I., Totaling, T., Straus, M.A., *The Dark Side of Families* (London: Sage Publications 1983) pp.17-18

place where an abuser feels in control. Violence in such cases may show his anger and frustration.

In many families, however, the abuse itself is all about the abuser wielding power over his victim. It is not necessarily that the day they first get married or start to live together he suddenly has all the power and she has none. Rather, each incident of domestic violence, be that physical abuse or emotional abuse, will be calculated to heighten the abuser's power. Each beating will teach her to 'behave' in the future. Each public embarrassment he creates will 'teach her not to show him up in the future'. So, in families where there is a great deal of difference in the levels of power between abuser and victim, it may simply mean that the abuse has been taking place for a long time.

Behind this theory there again lie cultural values. There are values which actually help to strip the victim of the power to fight back and which leave her particularly vulnerable. For example, it is often thought shameful for a woman to walk out on a husband. Many still think that the wife should look after the home and not have any income of her own but be entirely dependant on her husband.

Secondly, there is the norm that power should rest with the abuser. The male is 'the boss', the 'man of the house'. He is seen as the strong one in the relationship, the leader. When an abuser fails to measure up to that norm, either in reality or perhaps in his imagination, then he seeks a means to relieve tension and to reclaim his power. Or perhaps he feels that his victim is gaining too much power and he wishes to 'put her back in her place'. This violence, which is legitimated in society as a means appropriate for such an end, enters the family arena.

Power is, in itself, not a bad thing. The Bible is strewn with examples of men in powerful positions using their influence for good. There are also many stories of men without power who were nevertheless chosen by God for great tasks: Saul (1 Sam. 9 :21), David (2 Sam. 7 :18), Solomon (1 Ki. 3 :7) and Paul (1 Tit. 1 :15) to name a few. However, power can be misused. Also, striving towards power is a form of pride. It is the desire to set oneself over others. Being powerful is not a sin. Misuse of power, however, or pride in one's position, is in effect 'shaking the fist at God', declaring a self-sufficiency and rebelling against the humility promoted in biblical teaching.

In Matthew 18 :4, Jesus praises those who live with as little power as a child: 'Therefore, whoever humbles himself like this child is the greatest in the kingdom of heaven.' Proverbs 22 :4 makes clear the benefits of not seeking power and control: 'Humility and the fear of the LORD bring wealth and honour and life.' In reality it is neither the possession of power nor the lack of power (as referred to in the status inconsistency theory) which causes domestic violence. It is the tension which is caused when someone misuses power or refuses to accept a lack of power with humility and seeks to elevate himself via the oppression of others.

So far we have seen that there are many values held in our society which, when combined with social legitimization of violence, create the potential for violence to occur in a family. However, so far nothing has explained why violence will not occur in every family exposed to those values. Why is it that some families suffer domestic violence and others do not?

Contextual and situational factors

In answering these questions it is helpful to look at two aspects of domestic violence. Firstly, what is the context in which the violence takes place? In other words, what is the background, the general situation in which a family finds itself? The second issue is to identify the particular circumstances in which violence is likely to be perpetrated. To explain the distinction, let us take the example of Jack who travels to Africa and catches malaria. How did this happen?

Malaria is carried in tropical areas by mosquitoes infected with the disease – the situation in which the disease can be caught. So we can say that the 'contextual factors' for malaria are that the victim must be in a tropical area which has mosquitoes and those mosquitoes must be carrying malaria. However, thousands travel to infected areas all around the world each month and do not come back with malaria. So why does one unfortunate traveller get it whilst others do not?

To answer that question we must look at the specific circumstances of his case, the so-called 'situational factors.' In this case, Jack was foolish enough not to take preventative medicine before he left home. Then, when he was sleeping in a rough hut without a net, he was bitten by an infected mosquito. Those are the situational factors which caused him to get malaria. It has been argued by some that it must be the same with domestic violence. There are contextual factors, precursors if you like, which put a victim at general risk, and then situational factors which make her fall prone to that risk. So what are the *contextual factors* causing domestic violence?

The contextural factors do, of course, include the cultural norms which we have considered above. However, they also include individual characteristics of the abuser. This

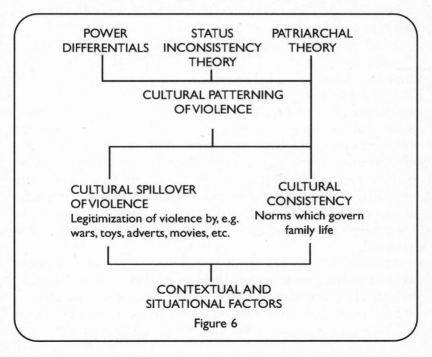

Figure 6

point is important because it emphasizes that abusers are still individually responsible for the violence. When we say that society legitimizes violence, that is not to say that abusers are just puppets of their cultural environment. In fact, they still have a choice to make about whether to be violent or not.

It has been found that men who abuse their wives often have low self-esteem and may tend towards feelings of vulnerability, helplessness, powerlessness and inadequacy. Other research shows that an abuser often believes in the traditional stereotyping of men and women, with a tendency to blame others for his actions, jealousy, a dual personality, poor responses to stressful situations and a belief that his violent behaviour should not have negative consequences for him.

Many, if not all, of these characteristics can be said to be sinful in the sense that they represent a state of separation from God – a 'fixed state in which men are trapped'. Of course, Christians are not immune from harbouring personality traits such as these; their existence in the life of a believer indicates areas in which the Holy Spirit has not been allowed to fully recreate the likeness of Christ.

Low self-esteem (which is different to humility) is incompatible with a Christian's calling to be 'a chosen people, a royal priesthood, a holy nation, a people belonging to God.' (1 Pet. 2 :9) Vulnerability, powerlessness, helplessness and inadequacy cannot be combined with a true and personal knowledge of God as an all-powerful father figure, involved and interested in the lives of his children. Jealousy is not God's chosen way either: 'A heart at peace gives life to the body, but envy rots the bones' (Pr. 14 :30). A belief that violence should not have negative consequences for the abuser indicates a failure to internalize the teachings of the Bible on violence and sin in general.

Cultural norms affect all families, except perhaps those very few who seek to cut themselves off in cults or tight religious communities. But not all families are affected by them in the sense that they become violent. However, it may be that abusers who have the above types of personality traits are more susceptible to the messages which encourage violence and may have a violent tendency inbuilt which is encouraged and legitimized by society. As we will see later, this consideration of the individual is very important when considering how to stop domestic violence, as it means we must focus on the individuals as much as on the general society.

So all this may help to explain why Fred abuses his wife but Stephen does not. How can we explain then why Fred abuses his wife some of the time but not at others? This is where *situational factors* come in. In fact, these factors are assumed by many to be the causes of domestic violence. In reality, whilst they play a large part, the problem is more deeply rooted. Situational factors are the problems which the family concerned may face at any given time. It may be a disagreement between the parties, perhaps over the children, or over where they should spend their holidays. Or, it could be something deep-seated – a general clash of personalities or attitudes to life which is festering beneath the surface of everyday life. It could be stresses caused by poverty or the unpredictable and unpleasant behaviour caused by one person misusing substances such as drugs or alcohol. In other words, situational factors are the day-to-day occurrences in family life which cause the 'flash points' at which violence then occurs.

Reinforcement

The argument so far, then, is that domestic violence is caused by the cumulative effects of cultural values, the cultural legitimization of violence and the individual characteristics of abusers when they combine in particular circumstances or situations. It is also useful, however, to look at how the pattern of violence is reinforced once it is started. There are two main theories to explain how this happens – intergenerational transmission and functionality.

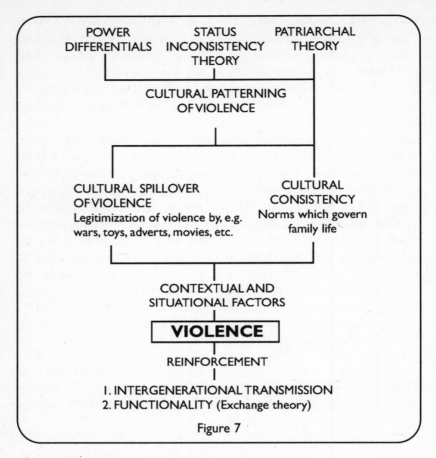

Figure 7

1. Intergenerational transmission

The theory of intergenerational transmission says that domestic violence is passed down in families like an old heirloom: from grandfather, to son, to grandchild. There is clear evidence that those who observe or experience family violence in childhood are likely to be involved in violent family relationships themselves. A study of four thousand abused women in New York City by Abused Women's Aid in Crisis Inc. found that over 80 per cent of abusers have a positive history of abuse in childhood or observed abuse against their own mothers. This intergenerational transmission can be simply explained in terms of an individual modelling his behaviour on that of a significant other. Of course, these brought up with such violence in the family perceive it as normal. In other words, it becomes legitimated as acceptable – a cultural norm. This legitimization is done in the specific context of the family, and a child growing up with violence may well come to accept, without doubt, the example set to him that violence is an appropriate and usual way of resolving family disputes. Of course, those disputes may well arise out of other values held by the father which are also passed to the son. So, if a son sees his mother regularly beaten for daring to be late with his father's dinner he may well grow up to think that a woman's rightful role is to provide for his needs. He may believe that he has every right to be annoyed if a woman puts her own life first, and that he can show that annoyance with violence. We have already discussed, in chapter 3, that this intergenerational transmission of violence is a 'perversion' of the biblical teaching of bringing up children in the way in which they should go.

2. Functionality of violence

Of course, if that violence generally succeeds in ensuring that the dinner is produced regularly for a period of time, then the next time there is a delay he will see violence as a good way to resolve the problem. In other words, abusers are violent because it works, because it achieves what they want – usually some kind of control over their victim.

Another aspect of this theory is that 'People hit and abuse family members because they can'.[12] If the costs of abusing a victim are low and the benefits high, then abusers will not think twice about being violent. The cost could be seen in terms of his victim's retaliation or response by leaving him. Or the costs could be social ones. If the violence has legal consequences, either civil or criminal, or if the violent behaviour is condemned by his peers and family, then the use of violence may be less attractive to the abuser. If the benefits of control and power exceed these costs, the violence will continue.

---

[12] Gelles, R.J. and Cornell, C.P., *Intimate Violence in Families* (London: Sage Publications 1985) p.120

So when all the theories are slotted together, a cyclical pattern emerges in which the combination of causal and reinforcing factors create a problem which, whilst it is one in which individual responsibility plays a large part, is nevertheless firmly rooted in our society. Fortunately, there are several potential 'break points' in this cycle and chapter 9 will look at just how the church can apply itself to using those break points to help families. First, however, it is necessary to look at what help is currently available and on what basis any further help the church offers should be given.

Five

What Help Can the Law Give?

Whether victims of domestic violence want to make a permanent split from their partners or whether they want to stay in the relationship but gain some respite from the violence, they would do well to seek legal advice on their situation. There are a wide range of laws which can assist and protect a person suffering from violence. Other laws apply to all instances of family breakdown, whether by reason of violence or not. This chapter gives a brief summary of the most relevant areas of law. It is important that each victim takes advice on how the law applies to her own individual situation. Also, the law in this chapter relates to England and Wales. The law is substantially the same in Scotland and Northern Ireland, although there are differences; victims in those, or other, countries should seek advice from a lawyer in their own area. Readers should also bear in mind that this chapter can only be a summary of the most frequently applicable parts of family law. If a given situation is not covered here it does not mean there is no legal remedy; advice should, again, be sought.

Ignorance of their options is an all too common reason why victims do not avail themselves of the help which is available to them. Whilst some will seek legal advice on the off chance that help will be available, others are reluctant to seek advice without being certain that there will be something a solicitor can do. Others are concerned about the costs of the consultation or the implications of taking a case through court.

This chapter, therefore, aims to give readers an overview of how the law can alleviate the suffering of victims and also addresses the question of legal costs. At the time of writing, matrimonial law is being radically changed by the introduction of the Family Law Act 1996. Whilst the Act was passed through Parliament in 1996, it requires pilot projects and the drafting of subsidiary legislation before it is fully implemented. It would appear that the provisions of the Act which deal with domestic violence will be in force by the time this book is published and, therefore, the section below deals exclusively with the law under this new Act. However, it appears that the law on divorce will take much longer to come into effect. This chapter, therefore, addresses both the old and the new law on divorce. Chapter 9 also touches on the opportunities which the implication of the new law in this area gives to the church for positive action.

Injunctions

The most immediate civil law action to protect a victim from domestic violence is an injunction. An injunction is the term for any court order which either prohibits a Respondent from doing something or else mandates that he should perform a specified act. Courts do have the power to make injunctions in any case. However, there is specific legislation dealing with domestic violence cases which is used in most instances. The original legislation dates back to 1976 but is now contained in the Family Law Act 1996.

In essence there are now two types of domestic violence injunctions – non-molestation orders and occupation orders.

1. Non-molestation orders

Non-molestation orders relate directly to the abuse of the victim. Molestation is a wide term which, in essence, covers any form of abuse or harassment against the victim. It clearly includes violence and the threat of violence. However, it also covers any other behaviour calculated to pester or upset the victim. Non-molestation orders have been obtained for fairly common behaviour such as verbal abuse, 'funny phone calls', repeated and unwelcome visits to the victim's house and so on. Other abusers have been more imaginative. In the leading case of *Horner v Horner*[1] the husband made frequent calls to his wife's place of work and hung posters on the school gates, addressed to the parents of her pupils and containing scurrilous remarks about her. In another case, *Spencer v Camacho*,[2] searching through the victim's handbag was held to be molestation. The case of *Vaughn v Vaughn*[3] sums up the wide definition of the term. In that case the court used the term molestation to refer to an abuser who 'made a perfect nuisance of himself to her the whole time'. Anything which disturbs the peace of the victim's life and distresses her or causes her worry or embarrassment is usually sufficient to be classed as molestation. It is important to note that actual violence is not a pre-requisite for a non-molestation order.

So, who can apply for a non-molestation order? The Family Law Act 1996 extends the group of potential applicants considerably, recognizing that domestic violence is a wide term which, sadly, affects people in a whole range of domestic settings. Anyone in the following groups can apply. (The term Respondent is used to refer to the person against whom the order is sought.)

1. Spouse – a person who has been, or is still, married to the Respondent.

2. Cohabitant – a person who has lived, or is still living, with the Respondent as man and wife.

---

[1] [1982] Fam.90; [1982] 2 AER 495
[2] (1983) 127 S.J. 155; 13 Fam.Law 114
[3] [1973] 1 WLR 1159; [1973] 3 AER 449

3. A person living in the same household as the Respondent, except someone who is only the Respondent's lodger, boarder, tenant or employee. In other words, anyone who shares a house with the Respondent but does not have a commercial relationship with him. This might include, for example, students sharing the same flat or a woman who has let a friend stay with her for free. This group will also include same-sex couples who do not fall into group two, since cohabitants must be male and female.

4. Relatives. This term is widely defined. It also includes people who would be relatives if cohabitants were actually married to each other. So, for example, if Sue and Jack are living together, Jack's father is treated as if he was Sue's father-in-law and so is classed as a relative.

5. People who are engaged to be married or who were engaged not more than three years before the case is brought to court. To fall within this group a victim must show evidence in writing of an agreement to marry, evidence of a gift of a ring in contemplation of marriage or a ceremony of engagement at which there were witnesses.

6. People who are parents of the same child or who have had parental responsibility for the same child.

7. People who are both parties to certain other family court cases, as defined by this Act.

Orders can also be obtained to protect a 'relevant child'. A 'relevant child' is:

1. A child who is living with either the Applicant or the Respondent or who might reasonably be expected to do so. So, a child who is away at boarding school at present or who is living with relatives because of the violence can be included in an order even though he or she is not actually living with the Applicant at the time the order is requested.

2. Any child whose interests the court thinks are relevant.

3. Any child who is the subject of certain kinds of court cases under the Children Act 1989. These include cases deciding with whom a child should reside or dealing with the amount of contact an absent parent should have with his child, and how such contact should work.

Any of these people can apply for an order – either as a free-standing application or as part of another court case.

The court also has powers to make orders in other cases as it deems appropriate, regardless of whether someone has actually asked for one. Orders can prevent molestation in general terms, can prohibit specific acts, or both. In making the order the courts must have regard to all the circumstances, including the need to secure the health, safety and well-being of the adults and children concerned. Orders can be made to last for a specific period or until a further order. If they are made in the context of another court case, the order will end if that case is withdrawn or dismissed.

2. Occupation orders

Occupation orders are orders which regulate who can live in a house. These are the orders a victim will seek when she needs to be able to live in her home without fear of her abuser returning, or when she needs to return to her own house but the abuser is refusing to allow her access. The law as introduced by the Family Law Act 1996 is more complicated than previously, and the nature of the remedy available depends very much on the rights the applicant has in regard to the house concerned.

It is beyond the scope of this book to explain all the different property rights the victim may have, and it will be important for a victim needing an occupation order to seek legal advice. She will have to explain who owns the house or in whose name the tenancy is. In some situations a victim can have an interest in a house even though her name is not on the deeds, and careful consideration must be given to a victim's position in those circumstances. For example, if a couple live together and buy a house, they may put it in his name only. On the face of it, she will not have an interest in that property. However, she may be able to show what is known as a beneficial interest if she contributed to the capital put down on the house or has made a subsequent capital contribution. If there is any doubt, legal advice should always be sought.

The law now divides applicants for occupation orders into five groups and the situation is slightly different for

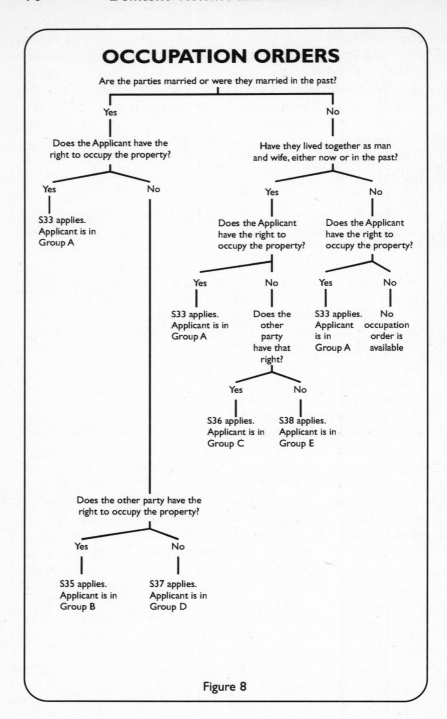

OCCUPATION ORDERS

Are the parties married or were they married in the past?

Yes

Does the Applicant have the right to occupy the property?

Yes — S33 applies. Applicant is in Group A

No

No

Have they lived together as man and wife, either now or in the past?

Yes

Does the Applicant have the right to occupy the property?

Yes — S33 applies. Applicant is in Group A

No — Does the other party have that right?

Yes — S36 applies. Applicant is in Group C

No — S38 applies. Applicant is in Group E

No

Does the Applicant have the right to occupy the property?

Yes — S33 applies. Applicant is in Group A

No — No occupation order is available

Does the other party have the right to occupy the property?

Yes — S35 applies. Applicant is in Group B

No — S37 applies. Applicant is in Group D

Figure 8

each of them. For ease of reference the flow chart in Figure 8 provides a simplified and visual version of the material which follows.

The following are five groups of applicants in the Act which I have lettered here for ease of reference.

Group A

Group A applicants are those who are entitled to occupy the home in question, either because they have a legal interest in the property, a beneficial interest, a contract or another Act of Parliament gives them the right to occupy it. It also covers those to whom the Family Law Act 1996 gives matrimonial home rights, namely spouses.

This group of people can ask for orders:

(a) to enforce their right to stay in occupation of the home

(b) to require the Respondent to let the Applicant back into the house or part of it

(c) to regulate the occupation of the home by either or both of the parties

(d) to suspend, restrict or prohibit the exercise of any rights the Respondent may have to occupy the house

(e) to restrict or terminate matrimonial home rights

(f) to require the Respondent to leave the house

(g) to exclude the Respondent from a defined area in which the house is included

When an application is brought by an applicant from Group A, the court must consider all the circumstances, including:

(a) the parties' respective housing needs and resources

b) the parties' financial resources

(c) the likely effect of the court's decision on the

health, safety and well-being of the parties and any relevant child

(d) the conduct of the parties.

An order granted to Group A applicants can last for a specified period, until a further order is made or until a specified event takes place, e.g. until the house is sold or until the parties are divorced.

Group B

A Group B applicant was once married to the Respondent but is now divorced and has no right to occupy what was the former matrimonial home, or the house which was intended to be the former matrimonial home. (This covers situations where a house was bought but the parties separated and did not live there together.)

When an order is made in favour of a Group B applicant, the order **must** include one of two provisions: 1) If the Applicant is actually in the house, even though she has no right to be there, then the order must say that the Applicant is not to be evicted from the house by the Respondent. 2) If she is not yet in the house then the order must say that she has the right to occupy the house for the period of the order and that the Respondent must let her in.

The order can also:

(a) regulate the occupation of the house by either or both parties

(b) prohibit, suspend, or restrict the exercise of the Respondent's right to occupy the property

(c) require the Respondent to leave the property

(d) exclude the Respondent from a defined area in which the house is included.

When granting an order to applicants in this group the court must consider:

(a) the housing needs and resources of the parties

(b) the financial resources of the parties

(c) the likely effects of the order on the health, safety and well-being of the parties and any relevant child

(d) the conduct of the parties

(e) the length of time which has passed since the parties lived together

(f) the length of time which has passed since the marriage was formally dissolved

(g) the existence of certain other types of court order, in essence, orders in relation to the ownership or sale of the house.

The orders granted to Group B applicants can only be for a limited period of not more than six months and cease on the death of either party. Only one extension is allowed, again for a maximum of six months.

Group C

Group C applicants are cohabitants, or former cohabitants, who do not have any right to occupy the house in which they once lived with the Respondent (or the house in which they intended to live together). If an order is made to an applicant in this group, then, again the order must contain the same two provisions as in Group B, either saying that the Applicant must not be evicted or saying that she has the right to occupy the house for the duration of the order.

The order can also:

(a) regulate the occupation of the house by both parties

(b) prohibit, suspend or restrict the exercise by the Respondent of his right to occupy the house

(c) require the Respondent to leave the house or part of it

(d) exclude the Respondent from a defined area in which the house is included.

The court must consider the following matters:

(a) the parties' respective housing needs and resources

(b) the parties' financial resources

(c) the likely effect of the court's decision on the health, safety and well-being of the parties and any relevant child

(d) the conduct of the parties

(e) the length of time the parties have cohabited

(f) whether the couple have had any children

(g) the length of time which has elapsed since the parties actually lived together

(h) the existence of certain other court proceedings.

Orders granted to Group C applicants cease on the death of either party. They must be made for a specified period of not more than six months and can be extended only once for a further period of not more than six months.

Group D

Group D applicants are those who are married to the Respondent but in a situation where neither spouse has the right to occupy the home in which they both live, or the house in which they used to live together. For example, this would cover spouses who were living with relatives.

Applicants in this group can obtain an order which will:

(a) require the Respondent to allow the Applicant to enter and remain in the house

(b) regulate the occupation of the house by both parties

(c) require the Respondent to leave that house

(d) exclude the Respondent from a defined area in

which the house is situated.

The court, when considering applications by people in this group, must consider:

(a) the parties' respective housing needs and resources

(b) the parties' financial resources

(c) the likely effect of the court's decision on the health, safety and well-being of the parties and any relevant child

(d) the conduct of the parties.

Again, an order in this group will be for a specified period of not more than six months with only one extension allowed of not more than six months.

Group E

The final group of applicants are those who are living as man and wife with the Respondent but in a situation where neither of them are entitled to occupy the house in question. For the purposes of this summary, the situation for Group D applicants is the same as for Group E. The differences between the two groups relate to the provisions, regarding the balancing test the court must apply in each case, between the harm to the Respondent in making the order and the harm to the applicant or a child in not making the order. These provisions are somewhat complex and thus have not been covered in this summary of injunctions.

Despite the complexity of these provisions, injunctions are emergency remedies. They can, if the situation is serious enough to warrant it, be made on an *ex parte* basis – that is without the other party being given notice of the first appointment. This has two advantages. First, the application can be made without having to wait for a court appointment to be allocated in often crowded lists. The application is simply squeezed into the lists as an 'extra' on

the day it is issued at court. This means that, if a solicitor
certifies the matter as urgent, the first hearing can often be
within a day or so of a victim seeking legal advice. The
second benefit is that an order can be made before the
Respondent even knows the matter is to go to court. This
obviously has serious implications, and so is reserved for
the most serious cases, where the victim is likely to be in
danger of violence if the Respondent is given notice of the
proceedings. An *ex parte* order is effective as soon as it is
served on the Respondent, so the Applicant is protected as
soon as he finds out that she has taken court action against
him. Cases which are brought on an *ex parte* basis are
always re-listed at court after a short time and the
Respondent is then given an opportunity to present his
case. Even if the case is not serious enough to warrant an
ex parte application, a certificate of urgency from a solicitor
will mean that the matter is listed more quickly than other
cases, and legal relief will still be relatively speedy.

Undertakings

It will still be open to a respondent to give undertakings
to the court. An undertaking is a solemn promise to the
court itself and is enforceable in the same way as an
injunction. An undertaking would usually be offered in the
same terms as the application. The advantage to the
Respondent is that, if an undertaking is accepted, there is
no finding of fact made against him by the court. In
essence, he is saying, 'I do not admit any of the allegations,
but I promise not to do anything in the future'. The
advantage to the victim is that it can prevent her having to
go through a contested hearing.

Enforcing undertakings and injunctions

At the end of the day, an injunction or an undertaking is
only a piece of paper. In many cases, it does the job; it
convinces the Respondent that he must now leave the
victim alone. In other cases, however, the order is
breached. What can the victim do then to enforce the court

order or the undertakings? There are two routes.

The first, and best, is the Power of Arrest. This enforcement will become more common under the Family Law Act 1996 since the Act allows it to be attached to orders more frequently than previously. If such a Power is attached, then the police can arrest for a breach of the injunction, even if the act complained of is not an arrestable criminal offence. To get a Power of Arrest there must have been violence or the threat of it – molestation alone is not enough. After an arrest for breach of the order, the abuser will be brought back to court within twenty-four hours. A Power of Arrest cannot be attached to undertakings and, indeed, the judge will not now be able to accept undertakings if he or she would be willing to attach a Power of Arrest to an order.

If there is no Power of Arrest, then it is up to the Applicant to apply to the court for a warrant for the arrest of the abuser. Once an abuser has been arrested, by either method, then the court has power to punish him for the breach of the order – the punishment is actually for a contempt of court and so the sentence may be different from a sentence for the same act in a criminal court. The court can fine and imprison and can suspend a sentence to give an abuser a second chance, if that is appropriate.

Divorce / judicial separation

Christian victims of domestic violence often struggle with the decision as to whether to divorce or not. Some feel that they are justified in doing so, while others feel that they would not oppose a divorce initiated by their partner but cannot conceive of starting one themselves. Yet others feel that whilst they need a formal separation, divorce is not the answer. In such cases, a judicial separation can often be the answer. The following case study (from my own practice) illustrates well the situation as it stands before the introduction of the Family Law Act 1996.

Pat was married to Sean and they had two children. He had been violent for a long time and she had eventually confided in a friend, who was also a church member. With the assistance of that friend she managed to leave her husband and now faced the question of how to move forward.

The grounds for divorce and separation are exactly the same and so, when she came to seek my advice, we started by discussing which of the grounds applied to her case. Many women cite adultery and for many Christians adultery is the only permissible ground for divorce. But, so far as Pat knew, her husband was not an adulterer. The obvious ground was thus her husband's unreasonable behaviour. The fact that he had been violent to her was sufficient to obtain a decree on this ground. It also meant that she could petition straight away as there is no waiting period for unreasonable behaviour, save that the parties must have been married for at least one year to obtain a divorce (this restriction does not apply to judicial separation).

Although this ground was obvious, I also discussed other options with her. Desertion is a ground which is available but little used, so our discussion focused on the other two grounds. Using two years separation (a ground which requires the Respondent's consent) would avoid the necessity to cite particular examples of behaviour in divorce papers. Often where the parties have already been apart a long time it can be a slightly less unpleasant alternative to unreasonable behaviour. Since Pat had decided she needed to make a formal break as soon as possible, it was not really necessary to consider the possibility of waiting still longer and using the ground of five years separation. The Respondent's consent is not needed for this ground. Previous Christian clients have said that they would not raise objections if their spouse divorced them on this ground (indeed, it is very difficult to prevent a divorce on this ground). These Christians have felt that it does not involve them conniving in untrue allegations against their spouses, or their being party to the decision to divorce against their principles.

Pat chose to use unreasonable behaviour, so we then went on to talk about whether she would choose a divorce or a separation. The advantage of a separation through the courts is that it does not end the marriage but does give both parties access to the wide-ranging powers of the court to sort out financial details of a family breakdown, where the parties cannot agree on a settlement. A separation also relieves the parties of their obligations to each other as man and wife. However, if either wanted to remarry in the future, they would have to then repeat the procedure and request a divorce. Pat decided that she did not want to retain any links at all with her husband, except for the children, so she opted for a divorce.

The first step was to prepare all the court papers. There is a petition setting out the details of the marriage and the ground for divorce and a statement of arrangements about the children. This form gives details about the children's accommodation, education, health and contact with the other parent. It gives the court enough information to decide whether it is obvious that it should make orders about the children, rather than leaving the parents to agree matters between themselves or refer the matter to court voluntarily. The marriage certificate also has to be filed at court. Pat had lost hers, so we obtained a copy from the local registry office. Pat signed all the papers and they were sent to the local county court.

The court processed the papers and Sean was served with them by post. He had 14 days to send back an acknowledgment form. He decided not to cooperate and refused to send it back. The solution was for us to send a bailiff to serve him with the papers personally, which then allowed the divorce to go ahead. Once we knew he had been served, Pat swore an affidavit, stating that the petition was still correct and that she wanted a divorce. Christians who object to swearing on the Bible can make a solemn affirmation instead. The papers were next looked at by a district judge – Pat did not have to attend court. The judge certified that she was entitled to a divorce. He also decided that there was no need to make an order about the children. Had he thought that this was necessary he could have ordered that the final divorce should not be given until the matters concerning the children were resolved.

As it was, the judge allocated a date in a few weeks time for Pat to be given her *decree nisi,* which is effectively the half-way stage in a divorce (although time wise it usually signifies that the divorce is nearly final). The decree nisi is needed before the court can make any final financial orders. Had she applied for a judicial separation, this would have been when the one decree of separation was given. The decree nisi was pronounced at court although, again, Pat did not have to attend. Six weeks and one day after the date of her decree nisi, Pat was able to apply for her *decree absolute*, which is the final decree of divorce and the one which actually dissolves the marriage. This application was done by post and the degree absolute came through a couple of weeks later.

Pat's case is typical of an uncomplicated divorce which, on average, takes about six months to work through the system. If the ground of adultery is used, then the co-respondent does not have to be named in the petition. If the co-respondent is named then he/she must also be served with the divorce petition, although not the form about the children.

Under the new law, introduced under the Family Law Act 1996, the procedure for getting a divorce will be somewhat different. However, at the time of publication it is likely to be at least one year, probably longer, before this new procedure is actually implemented. The steps will be as follows. (For the sake of clarity I have assumed throughout that the wife is the one who is divorcing her husband, although, obviously, the rules apply equally the other way around.)

1. Information meeting

Before the wife can start a divorce she must attend at an information meeting. The rules about exactly what must happen at such a meeting have, at the time of writing, not been finalized. However, the purpose of the meeting is for the wife to be given information about divorce to allow her to make an informed decision. It is thought that she will be told about the procedure, about the likely effects on the children and the availability of mediation and marriage counselling.

It is not necessary for the husband to go to a meeting just because his wife wants to divorce him. However, if he later wants to make an application about the children or the family finances, he too must go to a meeting – not necessarily the same one as his wife.

2. Statement of marital breakdown

The next step is for the wife to file a 'statement of marital breakdown' at the court. This cannot be done until three months have elapsed since she attended the information meeting. The statement is likely to be in a set form. It must contain the following:

(a) a statement that the marriage has broken down

(b) an indication that the person making the statement is aware of the purpose of the period for reflection and consideration (see below)

(c) an indication that the person making the statement wishes to make arrangements for the future.

The statement can be made jointly by both husband and wife, in which case both must have attended an information meeting. A statement cannot be filed until the parties have been married for one year.

3. Period for reflection and consideration

After the filing of the statement there follows a waiting period of nine months and 14 days. The purpose of this period is to allow the parties to reflect on whether the marriage can be saved and to have an opportunity to effect a reconciliation and also for them to consider what arrangements should be made for the future. The period is extended by six months if there is a child under sixteen or if either party requests an extension. It should be noted, however, that this extension does not apply if there is an occupation order or non-molestation order in force.

4. Application for divorce / separation

After the waiting period, the wife must make an application for divorce or separation. To do so she must make a declaration that, having reflected on the marriage breakdown and having considered the arrangements for the future, the marriage cannot be saved.

5. Arrangements for the future

At the same time as making the application for a divorce order, the wife must also show that the parties have resolved their financial arrangements. To do this, *one* of the following must be produced to the court:

(a) a court order dealing with finances (this could have been made by mutual agreement.)

(b) a negotiated agreement

(c) a declaration by the parties that they have made their financial arrangements

(d) a declaration by one party (with no objection from the other) that

(i) she has no significant assets and does not intend to make an application for financial provision and

(ii) she believes that the other party has no significant assets and does not intend to make an application for financial provision and

(iii) there are, therefore, no financial arrangements to be made.

6. Court consideration

When deciding whether to grant the divorce or separation, the court must make sure that all the above requirements have been met adequately. It must also consider whether there are any children about whom the court needs to make any orders.

There are, of course, other provisions contained in what are, in fact, rather complicated divorce laws. However, the above gives an adequate summary of the general procedure under the new law. It is interesting and encouraging that the Act sets out at the start, a list of principles on which the new divorce law is based. In that list it is specifically stated that 'any risk to one of the parties of a marriage and to any children of violence from the other party should, as far as reasonably practical be removed or diminished.'

The Act allows for regulations to be made, refining the operation of the general laws. No such rules have been made at the time of writing but it is anticipated that special rules may apply to victims of domestic violence.

Legal aid

Victims are often very worried about the cost of seeking legal advice, and this concern deters some from obtaining the protection which the courts could give them. For those on a low income, legal aid is likely to be available. There are two forms of legal aid for family cases. The first, known as the 'Green Form' scheme ('Pink Form' in Scotland), is an initial form of legal aid, available as soon as a form is signed in a solicitor's office. It is only available to those on a very low income or on certain welfare benefits, including income support and family credit. This scheme offers advice and correspondence only; it does not cover court proceedings except for divorce or judicial separation.

A fuller form of legal aid is then available for which the income and capital threshold is much higher. This aid has to be applied for and can be obtained on an emergency basis. Firms who hold a legal aid franchise have been tested on rigorous quality standards to enable them to run their legal aid services under a franchise. However, other firms also offer legal aid.

The full rules on legal aid cannot be explained here. If a victim is worried about costs, she should check when she makes the appointment whether she is likely to qualify and whether a short first interview will be given free. Many solicitors will do this. Some will even make the legal aid application for free as a 'loss leader' if need be. Victims should also ensure that the legal aid scheme is explained to them as, in some cases in which money or property is recovered or preserved, costs may be claimed back by the Legal Aid Board. Each case should be the subject of individual advice.

Financial cases

A victim who brings divorce or separation orders will often need to bring an application to court to deal with the family savings, income and often also the house. There are a wide range of powers available to the court to order that property be sold, or that it be transferred into the name of one party or the other – either for good, or until a certain event happens at which point it is to be sold. The court can order the payment of lump sums and maintenance for adults, although child maintenance must now (in most cases) be dealt with through the Child Support Agency. The courts must now also take into account pension funds as family assets, even if the parties are young and will not retire for some time.

Abusers will often try to make life hard for victims who are seeking such financial orders by not cooperating with the procedures and failing to provide information about their finances. Again, the courts have wide-ranging powers to force a party to give relevant information – the ultimate sanction is committal to prison for breaching an order of the court that the information be produced.

The situation for cohabitees is not so easy, since there are no special laws which deal with the finances of a family break-up if the parties are not married. They are dependant on the general property law, although there are still a range of orders which may bring cohabitees some financial relief. Cohabitees are not entitled to maintenance from a partner, although the rules on child maintenance are the same.

Again, it important that a victim who needs financial orders seek her own legal advice to find out exactly what can be done in her individual circumstances.

Welfare benefits

The welfare benefits system is complex, and it is impossible in a small section of a book like this to more than touch on welfare benefits. A victim leaving an abuser should seek advice from the benefits office as soon as possible. After separation she can claim on her own behalf and for children who are living with her. A single-parent allowance is available to parents who have been separated for over 16 weeks and who are going to remain separated. Income support is the most obvious benefit for those who are unemployed and looking after children, jobseekers allowance for those who are unemployed and able to work. However, others should not be forgotten: family credit (for those on a low wage and working over 16 hours per week), housing benefit (to help pay rent) and council tax benefit to name but a few.

Homelessness

Sadly, many victims of domestic violence who share a home with their abuser find that, in order to gain respite, they are forced to leave their home, either permanently or on a temporary basis. To a large extent this can be rendered unnecessary if a court order is obtained, forcing the abuser to leave the house instead. However, some victims believe that they will only ever get peace if they move away from the abuser. Others do not want their children to remain in a house where they witnessed parental violence. Some will be able to buy a house or to live with relatives. Others, though, will face homelessness if they flee violence at home.

The law covering their predicament is now covered by the Housing Act 1996. Under the Act, even if someone owns or rents a property, they are still homeless if it is not reasonable for them to continue to reside in it. The Act specifically states that it is not reasonable to continue to live in a house if it is probable that living there would lead to domestic violence against them or against someone who usually lives with them as a member of their family. In this context, domestic violence means violence from an 'associated person ' (which was dealt with earlier in the chapter) or threats of violence.

So, if a victim is fleeing domestic violence and wishes to be rehoused, what must her local authority do to help her?

It depends whether she is in a priority need category. Priority needs are:

■ a pregnant woman or someone who lives with her

■ a person with dependant children

■ a person who is vulnerable as a result of old age, mental illness, handicap or physical disability or other special reason, or with whom such person resides

■ a person who is homeless as a result of an emergency like fire or flood.

Many victims will have children whom they intend to take with them and will clearly have a priority need. Victims who are childless, however, may argue that as a result of the violence itself they are vulnerable because of 'other special reason', but domestic violence alone is not specifically stated to give rise to priority need.

If a victim appears to be in a priority need, the local authorities have a duty to provide accommodation whilst they deal with an application for rehousing. If, after looking at the case, they accept that a victim does have that priority need and is homeless, then they have a duty to 'secure that accommodation is available for occupation for the applicant'. However, this need not mean that they give the victim a council house. If they are satisfied that there is other accommodation in the area (in effect, privately rented accommodation) which would be suitable for the applicant, then they only have a duty to give advice and assistance to help the victim rent one of those houses.

This duty only runs for two years. After that, the case must be reviewed so that the council can decide whether to continue to make the property available. It will continue to be available only if the applicant has a priority need at the time of review and there is no other suitable accommodation available in the area.

If, on her first application, a victim is not classed as having a priority need, then the local authority's only duty is to give advice and assistance to help her get accommodation.

It is also worth noting that a local authority can refer an applicant to another local authority, if the applicant has a connection there. However, this cannot be done if the applicant or someone who will live with her will run the risk of domestic violence in that district. So, if Sue lives in Bristol but wishes to make a fresh start well away from her abuser, she could request rehousing in, say, Liverpool. Normally the local authority could pass her application back to Bristol. However, if she would still be at risk of violence if she lived anywhere within the Bristol area, Liverpool must rehouse her.

Criminal Law

Domestic violence often involves the commission of criminal offences. Spouses and cohabitees are just as protected by the criminal law as those who are assaulted by strangers. Later chapters will discuss the pros and cons of using the criminal law to deal with domestic violence and the services offered to victims by the police. However, it may be useful for victims to know at this stage some of the relevant criminal charges which can be brought.

1. Common assault

Common assault is the most minor of assault charges. It covers situations where violence is not actually committed, but the victim is caused to apprehend the immediate infliction of unlawful violence. So, a threat to batter a woman at some point in the future would probably not come under this heading. However, if an abuser is waving a fist or a weapon in her face and threatening to use it on her, that would amount to an assault. Common assault also covers the intentional or reckless infliction of force.

2. Actual bodily harm

(Section 47 Offences Against the Person Act 1861)
For this offence to be committed, an abuser must

intentionally or recklessly cause the victim to fear immediate infliction of unlawful violence and cause actual bodily harm (ABH). ABH involves more than merely touching someone, but a bruise might be sufficient harm to bring a charge of ABH.

3. *Wounding or inflicting grievous bodily harm*

(Section 20 Offences Against the Person Act 1861)

For this offence to be committed, an abuser must unlawfully and maliciously wound or inflict grievous bodily harm (GBH) on his victim, either with or without a weapon. A wound requires a breaking of the skin whilst grievous bodily harm means harm which is 'really serious'. Obviously, broken bones or severe internal injuries would come under this heading.

4. *Wounding or causing grievous bodily harm with intent*

(Section 18 Offences Against the Person Act 1861)

For this offence the abuser must have caused the wound or GBH with intent either to do some GBH or intending to prevent the lawful detaining of someone. This is the most serious of these offences and can carry a maximum sentence of life imprisonment.

When the police are called out to a domestic violence incident, they often take advantage of other offences to remove the abuser from the property, at least temporarily. For example, the police may find that he is being drunk and disorderly or causing a breach of the peace. Often an abuser will have outstanding warrants of arrest for other offences (including possible unpaid fines) for which they can arrest, even though that was not the reason they came to the house. If an abuser is foolish enough to turn on the police, he might be arrested for assault on a police officer. Criminal damage is another possible offence for which an abuser may be arrested.

For those who have suffered injuries as a result of a criminal assault, it is possible to make a claim for compensation from the Criminal Injuries Compensation

Board. Compensation is awarded on a tariff basis, depending on the injuries sustained and is available to victims of domestic violence so long as it can be shown that the abuser will not benefit from the money. It would, therefore, be almost certain that a victim would have to have left her abuser with no intention to reconcile with him. The usual conditions of the scheme apply – for example, to get a payment the victim must report the offence to the police and cooperate fully with them. Many victims choose not to cooperate, however, not wanting to involve the criminal justice system beyond getting initial police protection.

The law is not always a perfect system. Some victims feel that the law is powerless to give them real protection from violence. In other cases, injunctions are extremely effective.The fact is, that in all cases, there will be some legal remedy open to a victim which may well alleviate her problems, if it does not solve them completely. It is always worth seeking initial legal advice. Then at least a victim who chooses not to take legal proceedings will do so from an informed position.

Six

Service Providers: Sources of Help

> I'd have got out years ago if only I had realized there were people who could help me. I thought I was trapped with no way out.

So spoke a victim of domestic violence who suffered in silence for many years simply through ignorance of the services open to her. Domestic violence service provision has mushroomed in recent years as the issue has been publicized and as more public money, sometimes from European funds, has been made available to assist victims. Agencies which started out as small groups of concerned women working out of their own homes have become national organizations or very effective local groups. However, there are still two basic problems concerning domestic violence provision.

Firstly, money is limited. Many agencies are charity-based and largely dependant on fund-raising. Even social service departments are hampered by budgetary constraints. This constraint is particularly striking in the realm of service provisions for male victims. Whilst some research has been done on male victims (for example by Audrey Macklin at Liverpool John Moores University), the statistics and information about male victims are nowhere near as abundant as those for female victims. Agencies with limited funds are often reluctant to place money into services where only a limited number of victims would appear to benefit, when there is documented greater need elsewhere. However, those seeking increased provision for male victims would argue that if there are no services available for men then male victims will not come forward – and so a vicious circle is formed.

The second problem is a linked one – that of making victims aware of the existence of services. Since budgets are often so limited, money is not readily available for advertising. In addition, there is the problem of reaching victims whose abusers often keep them in isolation. This means that victims may not attend women's groups or social centres where information is available. Increasingly, emphasis is being put on publicity campaigns which have a dual purpose. Firstly, they proclaim very publicly that domestic violence is not acceptable. Secondly, they try to make victims aware of the availability of services for them and of the fact that they need not suffer in silence.

However, these campaigns, such as the media-based Zero Tolerance campaign, are faced with similar issues to those seeking to work with male victims. There is real concern that if such campaigns are successful, large numbers of victims will approach service providers who, with their limited resources, will become swamped. To be turned away, or given inadequate or inappropriate assistance because of oversubscription, could be very harmful to a victim and could even result in her not seeking further help but returning to her abuser. However, it is difficult to increase the available service capacity prior to a campaign, since money is often allocated based on existing statistics of current service users. Again, a vicious circle can form.

All this notwithstanding, there are many agencies able to offer help to victims. Some of these agencies are nationally based while others are local groups, perhaps church based, unique to a particular area. A church wishing to help victims of domestic violence will need to be able to identify both the needs which a victim may have and the agencies in the locality which can meet those needs if the church itself cannot assist. There is no substitute for meeting with agencies in the area to find out specifically what is available in a given locale. Often one agency will be able to give names of other agencies who can help – until a full picture emerges. If a church is able to offer a quality service which can bolster existing provision, then most agencies will be interested to meet with church people to exchange information so that they themselves can refer to the church as and when appropriate.

The following case study gives an indication of a victim's typical needs and the kind of groups and agencies that can help. The case is fictional, created to include as many agencies as possible. However, it remains true to the reality of domestic violence cases.

Imagine that Suzanne approaches you after a church service. She is a member of your church and is worried about her sister, Karen. Karen attended church as a child but when she married she stopped going. She used to be a shop assistant but also stopped working when she married John. They now have three children. Sam is a very independent thirteen-year-old who is very close to his dad. The twins, Shelly and Alex, are younger, aged six. John and Karen own their own house, subject to mortgage, and John is employed as a manager in a local carpet factory. Suzanne is worried because she suspects that Karen and the children are being abused. Karen now rarely contacts her sister, who is her only living relative. However, on several occasions when they have met, she has seen bruises on Karen and also on one of the twins. She questioned Karen about this. Karen would only say that things were 'hard' at home but then became anxious and left. Suzanne has now heard through a mutual acquaintance that Karen was in hospital recently with broken bones. This acquaintance has a child in the same class as the twins and has commented that the twins are often off school. Suzanne wants the church to help her sister. Suzanne herself is an assistant hotel manager and, having just been relocated, is living temporarily in one of the hotel rooms.

Initial approaches

This story raises many different issues. The very first, however, is that this story is being told by Suzanne and not Karen herself. It certainly sounds like Karen is being abused. However, this may not be the case; the bruises may be accidental. Her isolation from her sister may be due to busyness, a family argument or other reasons which Karen has chosen not to explain to Suzanne. The point is that it is easy to make assumptions when dealing with domestic violence – assumptions that someone is a victim at all; assumptions about what has happened to an individual; assumptions about why the abuser has done it; assumptions about what the victim needs and how she can best be helped. In attempting to assist a victim it is essential to avoid a paternalistic attitude which seeks to take over the life of a vulnerable person and to direct it 'for her own good'. However well-intentioned, this attitude itself is a form of abuse.

A victim is her own person and what help she accepts is entirely up to her. She may decide to remain with a horrifically abusive partner. That is her choice. She may prevaricate over what seems to the helper to be the most straightforward decisions. However, the fine line between encouragement and persuasion or coercion should not be crossed. All available help should be offered to a victim, but it is up to her whether to accept it or not. By all means give a victim the knowledge she needs to make an informed choice, but do not deny her that choice. Nor should any adverse inference be drawn from a refusal to accept help. It does not mean that a victim is undeserving or ungrateful and so should be denied help in the future. It may simply be that she is unable to cope with a change in her life at that time, that she lacks the strength, or that she is waiting for a more opportune time. She may be persuaded by fear or guilt. None of this means that she will not take up help in the future. It is therefore vital that help is offered on a long term-basis to a victim, not something which is forced on her or offered on a 'take it or leave it' basis.

In this particular case, careful thought would have to be

given as to how you should approach Karen. It should go
without saying that church workers, in whatever area they
approach an individual, should be sensitive and respectful
of the individual's own privacy and beliefs. However, in this
case, one must also consider Karen's safety. You may be
tempted to write her a friendly letter:

> Dear Karen,
>
> I hope you do not mind me writing to you. I am a leader in
> Suzanne's church and she has asked me to contact you. She
> has mentioned that you may be having some problems at
> home with which we may be able to help. I do not wish to
> interfere but write merely to let you know that if you need
> help we are here. Please feel free to contact me . . .

Such a letter may seem innocuous. The contents could be
put into a similar phone call. However, what if John opens
Karen's mail? What if she hides the letter and he finds it?
What if he listens in to her conversations on the phone?
Even such a vague and innocuous approach may get her
into serious trouble. Imagine John's reaction. If he is
abusive to her he is also likely to be controlling and to want
to keep her in isolation. He may ask her: what has she been
saying about him? To whom has she been talking? Violence
may well follow such a discovery. Discretion must be used
in each case and a different approach may be appropriate
in each case. However, generally it will be best to get
information to the victim in a form which will not endanger
her. Here Suzanne might be able to find a time to pass a
verbal message on to Karen.

Confidentiality

The second issue which the case study raises is that of
confidentiality. If Karen gets in touch and asks for your
help, then Suzanne may well be anxious to know how her
sister is getting on and what progress is being made.
However, a victim's revelations to you and the nature of the
help given to her must always remain confidential. No

information should be given to anyone, without the victim's express consent. This confidentiality is particularly important in domestic violence cases, where an abuser may be seeking to trace a victim who has gone into emergency accommodation.

Of course, issues of confidentiality are never clear-cut. For example, what should you do if you know that the children are being abused and she refuses to do anything about it? What should you do if she confesses that she feels suicidal? These are issues which must be resolved as a matter of policy before work with victims is started. Some agencies will set out boundaries at the very first meeting with a victim. They may tell the victim that everything will remain confidential unless they have reason to believe a child is in danger, or that the victim may harm herself. In those circumstances they would seek the victim's permission and cooperation in alerting appropriate agencies first, but may have to break confidentiality in those very limited circumstances. That way, the victim can choose not to reveal information which may have to be disclosed. If, in conversation, it appears that she is about to make such a disclosure then a reminder at that point may be appropriate.

> Let us assume that Karen herself gets in touch with you. When you meet she admits that she is being both emotionally and physically abused. Just last night she was assaulted and she shows you considerable bruising around her ribs. She also tells you that the children have been hit on several occasions. She does want to get out of the violent home but doesn't know where she can go or how she would survive. She is concerned about losing her children, both to social services and to her husband whom she fears may keep them and refuse to allow her contact with them. She asks you to get her as much help as you can.

In some cases, victims will only ask for a very limited form of help and care must be taken not to try to give more assistance than the victim is prepared to accept. Here, however, you have been given carte blanche to help Karen. She will take as much help as is offered to her. The question is – what kind of help does she need and what help is available? The availability of services will differ from town to town, but the suggestions given here are general ones and should apply in most areas. If a certain form of help is not available, this need may indicate an area in which a local church could give specific help to victims. The needs, however, of someone in Karen's situation will be common to most victims.

Medical needs

Since Karen has been assaulted recently, one of the priorities is to obtain medical advice. Injuries can often be less than obvious, particularly with blows to the head. Also, whilst not essential, a record of attendance at a GP's surgery or hospital emergency department for injuries can assist in later legal action, if any is to be taken. Often victims do not wish to tell their doctor exactly how the injury occurred and, again, this is not essential.

Emergency protection

Chapter 5 describes the kind of emergency legal protection which is likely to be available to a victim. Experience working with victims or the recommendations of others in the field should enable you to locate a solicitor who is used to dealing with domestic violence cases and who has a reputation for expertise in the area of family law. Another sign of a quality solicitor is if the firm holds a Legal Aid Franchise in Family Law. This distinction means that they have been audited by the Legal Aid Board on a regular basis and have passed quality checks. However, not every good solicitor has applied for a franchise so it is not an exclusive sign of quality. Membership in the Solicitor's Family Law Association (SFLA) might indicate a solicitor who will not take an unduly aggressive approach to family cases. It is advisable to seek legal advice as soon as possible, even if the victim decides that no immediate action is to be taken.

Emergency accommodation

Karen has told you that she wishes to leave John as soon as possible, at least until she feels safe to return to him. How is her leaving best to be achieved? One possibility is to see if a court order can be obtained, ordering John to vacate the family home so that Karen and the children can return. Again, this procedure is covered in chapter 5. This option can be of great benefit to the children, since they will not suffer further by being summarily moved from their usual and familiar home environment. However, it may well be that this will take several days, even if the order can be obtained. What about those few days? She may be able to get a court order protecting her from the violence at once. That way she will be protected for the few days it will take to get John out of the house. Her sister Suzanne has no accommodation and there are no other friends or relatives who can help.

The answer will almost invariably be to approach a local refuge. These refuges may be independently run, and can often be located through police or social services (see below). However, many are run by the national Women's Aid organizations – there is one for Scotland, England, Wales and Northern Ireland. See Appendix 1 for addresses and contact numbers. If the local group is unknown to you, the national enquiry lines will be able to give you local numbers.

Women's Aid groups are usually, but not exclusively, affiliated to the national organizations. They exist to help abused women and offer a range of services which will be mentioned throughout this case study. One of these services is the provision of a refuge facility.

Refuges are safe houses. The network throughout the nation means that if space is not available in a local refuge, accommodation can often be found elsewhere. The addresses are secret and the houses secure. Sometimes male children over a certain age are not admitted, so the possibility of Sam joining his mother and the twins would have to be checked. Refuges do involve an element of communal living, although each family is usually able to have its own bedroom, even if this space is often cramped. Other rooms are shared. Whilst the accommodation will not be like living at home, there will be informal support and companionship available from others in the refuge. Also, most refuges offer a strong formal support programme to meet the other needs of the victim. Some refuges are catered, others expect each family to cook for itself. There is usually no limit on the length of a victim's stay (or indeed, the number of times she returns to a refuge) although, obviously, most victims will want to find more suitable accommodation for the long term.

In some areas, particularly those with a significant ethnic minority population, there are special refuges offering services to a particular segment of the community. For example, **Solas Anois** offers a service to London-Irish women. In Liverpool the **Amadudu Refuge** offers service to black women and white women with black children. They have accommodation tailored to the needs of Moslem women and a translation service for several languages.

Another possibility is that a victim could be given accommodation in a homeless hostel. Often this option is used by social services in areas where there is no local refuge facility. The issue of the church offering accommodation in these circumstances is discussed in chapter 9.

Retrieval of belongings

Having found Karen a safe bed for the night, you may find that she is without all but the most basic of possessions. If the house is in joint names she has a perfect right to return to the house to collect items. Where couples are married but the house is only in the name of one spouse, say the husband, then the other spouse has a right of occupation in the house anyway, so long as they remain married. Karen, therefore, can break in if necessary – for example, if she has not got her keys or if her husband has changed the locks. It goes without saying that care should be taken when returning. It may be that there is a safe time when you can accompany her. However, in these circumstances the police are usually very helpful in providing an escort to the property.

Immediate financial needs

Since Karen is not working, an immediate application should be made for welfare benefits. Again, **Women's Aid** centres usually have workers who are able to assist with application forms. However, this is an area where the church can easily offer help. Income support would be available to Karen in this situation. It is also worth noticing that domestic violence would qualify her to make an application for a social fund grant or loan (once she has been on income support for a certain length of time) so that she can obtain items requiring capital, such as furniture once she is rehoused. Grants are discretionary, however. Housing benefit is likely to be available to cover her immediate housing costs and can be claimed to give to a refuge as rent.

Long-term housing / financial needs

Again, legal advice, which for Karen would be available on legal aid, should be sought. Since she is married, the court has wide powers to give her capital and maintenance which may improve her long-term finances. (Interim maintenance can often be obtained under a court order, requiring John to cover at least her basic needs before a final financial settlement is reached.) Also, if she is considering returning to employment, full welfare benefits advice should be sought to see how her benefits would be affected. It is usually advantageous for a claimant to work and, indeed, benefits such as family credit, payable to parents working more than sixteen hours a week, are a positive encouragement for single parents to work.

Chapter 5 has already covered the law on rehousing. An application for new accommodation can be made via the local council housing office who should consider a domestic violence case sympathetically. Since she is a house owner, she will probably be required by the council to obtain a letter from a solicitor. This letter usually has to confirm that she is seeking legal help as a result of domestic violence, and what the situation is with regards to her house. The rationale behind this requirement is that it prevents those wanting to be rehoused claiming falsely that they are victims in order to circumvent waiting lists and rules on rehousing. Often victims become alarmed as it appears to them that unless they give up their house they will not be entitled to a council house. If they have equity in their house this can be a difficult decision. In practice, with the intervention of a solicitor, accommodation can usually be obtained even if the victim has an ongoing claim to her house.

Also, it is worth the church being aware of the local housing agencies in the area since they are often able to provide permanent accommodation, either more speedily than the local authority, or else of a better quality – often both. Again, housing benefit may be available to pay a private landlord.

Criminal proceedings

Karen has been assaulted. She may, therefore, wish to press criminal charges against John. Many areas now have specialist **Police Domestic Violence Units (DVUs)** who are able to give specialized service to victims. They are often short-staffed and will cover every domestic violence incident in their area. Nevertheless, the understanding and commitment to helping domestic violence victims which officers in these units have often means that by dealing with the unit a victim will receive a better service than by merely dealing with a uniformed officer. A DVU officer will be able to explain the criminal process, giving detailed information not only about how the system works, but also about what it will be like for the victim at various stages in the process. They will be able to evaluate the likely outcome of a given case so that a victim can better assess whether she wishes to go ahead. They are likely to keep records of assaults so that, even if no action is taken at the present time, a full picture can be given to the court at a later date. Again, Karen should be given a full choice about whether or not to proceed.

If she does go ahead, she will have to deal with the stress and uncertainty of going to court and, perhaps, giving evidence if the case is defended. It may well be that the church can support her through this process. If not, **Women's Aid** groups often offer a 'court support service', as do **Victim Support.** Victim Support is a national charity with over 370 local offices. They have trained volunteers who offer support to all victims of crime. The police often refer to Victim Support (with a victim's consent), but victims can simply contact the service themselves. Whilst Victim Support is a general organization dealing with all types of crime, they do have a nationally agreed Code of Practice for dealing with cases of physical, sexual, emotional and mental abuse of women by male partners or ex-partners. Court support services typically provide a volunteer to attend with a victim at the court hearing, both for emotional support and to give practical information where needed.

Alarm systems

The most vulnerable of women are often very afraid of repeat attacks, either in their new homes or in the streets, perhaps whilst picking the children up from school or attending another venue where abusers would be able to trace them. In some areas personal alarms are available. Again, this is very much dependant on funding, and the rules concerning who is able to have an alarm are often very stringent. For example, it may be that alarms are not available if a woman has a phone or if she is still living with her abuser, as it would be too easy for him to tamper with the machine. Sometimes the loan of alarms is time-limited so that other women can have the benefit of them. Some alarms are installed in houses, operating via a push-button system. In other schemes mobile phones have been loaned, free of charge, to victims. They are programmed for outgoing calls to the police only and give protection wherever a victim is. In cases of extreme violence and continued vulnerability it is worth enquiring with local **police** and / or **Women's Aid** groups who, if they do not themselves distribute alarms, are still likely to know whether they are available in the area.

Long-term emotional needs

Karen, like every victim, is likely to have long-term emotional needs. The church may well be able to assist her with these needs. Another prime source of help is, again, **Women's Aid.** Whilst precise services vary from group to group, depending on funding, it is common for Women's Aid groups to provide counselling services, both for long- and short-term sessions.

Women's Aid often have self-help groups which aim to bring together women in similar situations and with shared experiences to strengthen each other and to help each other to begin new lives. These groups can often be extremely effective in helping victims overcome the effects of isolation and in helping them build up a new network of friends. A variety of activities is planned according to the needs and desires of the members, and these can help victims learn new skills and achieve a fresh self-confidence.

Many Women's Aid groups also have outreach workers

whose function is to 'befriend' women who either remain in a violent home or who have been rehoused and are starting again. These workers can be a useful link between a Women's Aid centre and a victim who is beginning to strike out alone. Services at Women's Aid are generally free of charge. Counselling is also available from private counselling agencies. It is wise to check on a counsellor's accreditation and experience in dealing with domestic violence. It can also help to check their prices and policy on confidentiality before a commitment to counselling is made. Further information can be obtained from the addresses listed in Appendix 1.

Children

Of course, in dealing with Karen's case, the children's needs should not be forgotten. Indeed close attention should be paid to them, as domestic violence can have severe effects on even very young children.

Let us assume, for this case study, that Karen goes into a refuge with the twins. However, Sam wants to stay with his father and refuses to go with her, even though the refuge would allow him to stay there. John wants all three children to stay with him whilst Karen wants Sam to come to join her and the twins.

Most refuges have services geared to children – where money permits, a children's worker is employed. Scottish Women's Aid describes the function of such a worker as follows.

> She supports and works with children and their mothers and acts as the children's advocate – enabling them to speak and helping them to achieve their rights. With the support of a children's worker children can work through their own feelings at their own pace. They need to talk about what has happened, how they felt about the abuse of their mother, and often talk of their own abuse. Through talking children day by day reveal more about what they saw or felt, often when describing their nightmares or describing a picture. They

are supported to see that it is wrong to abuse and helped to work out their anger and mixed feelings about the abuser. Also they can shout, laugh and play, be messy and have fun, usually including play sessions, trips and outings, spend time with children, focusing on their needs, exploring their feelings and much more! The work ranges from one-to-one work to group work, and all the children and women are involved in working towards an abuse free, anti-violence, anti-discriminatory atmosphere.[1]

So, when Shelly and Alex are in the refuge, it is likely that there will be a worker to help them come to terms with the situation and to begin work with them. However, Women's Aid often provide a similar service to children who leave a refuge and for those, like Sam, who never go to one. In Scotland, two-thirds of Women's Aid groups also offer a children's outreach work which tends to consist of summer play schemes, after-care support groups and sometimes one-to-one work with children. Their ability to offer the full service they would like to children is, again, hampered by lack of funding.

In some areas, however, other agencies also provide children's groups. These can be run by national charities such as the **NSPCC** and **Save the Children.** Information about local programmes should be obtainable from national offices – see appendix 1 for addresses and numbers. Social services are able to make provisions in other areas. This is especially so where children are particularly traumatized and may benefit from seeing a child psychologist.

In this case study, Karen will also have to consider what action she wishes to take if John has been abusing the children. Again, she will wish to take full legal advice both from police family support units (the part of the police service which deals with child abuse cases) and from a solicitor, so that she is aware of all her options. She need not fear having her children taken away from her simply because she admits that they were abused in the past. Care proceedings will only be taken where the children are in

---

[1] Scottish Women's Aid, *Children – Equality and Respect* (1994) p.10

current danger or there is a likelihood of future danger. So, taking them away from the abusive home can alleviate the harm to the children. However, a failure to protect children can be significant in legal proceedings and so she will want to be fully advised.

If Karen has continuing concerns about Sam, or indeed the twins, and wants confidential advice, an additional service is the **NSPCC Child Protection Helpline.** This helpline gives a service for anyone, including children, concerned about any form of child abuse. It is described as,

> A free, twenty-four hour direct service which provides counselling, information and advice to anyone concerned about a child at risk of abuse throughout England, Wales and Northern Ireland.

The line is staffed by trained counsellors who are also social workers and experienced in child protection issues. Calls can be made without giving identifying details, although if such details are given then the NSPCC will make contact with social services or the police. Of course anyone genuinely worried about a child can also contact their local social services children and families section.

Karen may well have to deal with a dispute over where the children should live and on what terms the non-resident spouse should see the children. Legally, the terms familiar to most people, 'custody' and 'access', were changed some years ago to 'residence' and 'contact'. It is possible for both Karen and John to apply to a court for a contact or residence order to end any dispute. Again, a good solicitor will try to resolve such issues by negotiation, but the courts are there as a last resort. A history of domestic violence is taken into account when the court makes its decision and the children's welfare, not the parent's wishes, will be the paramount consideration. Here we are told that Sam is an intelligent and independent thirteen-year-old who seems to be voicing his own opinions about where he should live. In all cases, the ascertainable wishes and feelings of the children are taken into account, usually through a court welfare officer who talks to the children. The older a child becomes, the more weight is attached to his opinions.

However, the children's wishes are only one of a range of factors a court must consider – and it must be remembered that children do not always know what is best for them. Also, generally, courts dislike separating siblings, although on occasions it has to be acknowledged that, on the facts of a particular case, to split them up is in fact the best arrangement.

What if one or more of Karen's children does end up living with John? Karen may well have a range of feelings which could be hard for her to face. She may have on-going concerns about their safety, guilt at splitting the family up, perhaps even a mixture of love and – especially in Sam's case – a feeling that they have rejected her and chosen their father instead. She may feel that not having her children with her is another part of the abuse, and that the legal system has let her down. Clearly the church ought to be able to offer a supportive role in such cases. However, there are two organizations which also offer support to parents separated from their children. **Families Need Fathers** is a very vocal and politically active group. They describe themselves as, 'a voluntary self-help society which provides advice and support on children's issues, for separated, divorced and unmarried parents'. They have a quarterly magazine and a network of recommended local services. A similar organization is **Mothers Apart from Their Children (MATCH)** which offers similar services. The addresses for both groups can be found in appendix 1.

If one or more of the children are not to live with Karen, she may need assistance with the arrangements for contact. It is possible that she will not feel safe collecting the child directly from John, and a third party may have to become involved. This third party is often a family member, but in this case there may be no-one available. Specific ways in which a church can help with the practical aspects of contact sessions are discussed in detail in the final chapter.

At some stage, whilst you are helping Karen, John approaches you. He says that he understands that you are helping Karen, that he is sorry about what has happened and that he wants to try again. He asks for your help.

Now new issues will be raised and old ones put into a different context. Firstly, there is the issue of confidentiality. John says that he understands that you are assisting Karen. But does he really know that or is he testing you to try and find out information? Of course, you will not want to be untruthful, nor will you want to turn John away, but great care must be taken not to reveal information about Karen without her consent. Secondly, are you able to help both Karen and John? Lawyers have frequent ethical problems relating to a concept known as 'conflict of interests'. A lawyer in this situation would only represent either Karen or John. They could not represent both because their underlying interests are different. For lawyers, this is a matter of professional conduct as set out in regulations.

You, of course, as a representative of the church, will not be acting under such formal restrictions. Nevertheless, it is an issue which you should consider when faced with this situation. Let us assume Karen gives you her permission to let John know that you are in fact helping her. You will then want to discuss with her how she feels about you meeting with John. She may feel that is a good idea, that you can be an intermediary, passing on messages. That, however, is a much more limited role than being a helper to John as he has requested. If that is all she is prepared to let you do, then you will have to explain the situation to John. Obviously, you will wish to avoid double-handedness and deceit. There could be no question of you trying to help John behind Karen's back – advising her on a course of action, for example, simply as a form of persuasion that will help John.

If Karen will only consent to you having a limited role with John, however, that leaves you in a quandary. Suppose he is genuine. What if he really is sorry and wants to make amends? If you helped him, then perhaps the family could be put back together. Even if reconciliation were not the outcome, is he still not entitled to assistance from the church? Should not the church be open to everyone, not just those who arrive first? It is worth considering how you are going to deal with this problem at the outset of your work with victims of domestic violence, as it most certainly

will arise at some time. A solution may be to allocate
another worker within the same church to help John whilst
you carry on your work with Karen. You could agree that
information will not be passed between the two workers
unless Karen and John agree. Two solicitors in the same
firm cannot do this as all knowledge is taken to be available
to all within the firm. However, there is no reason why the
church should face such a problem. The important thing is
that both John and Karen know the boundaries within
which you are operating and are comfortable with them.

You will note that when referring to John above, I
deliberately used the term 'if he is genuine'. Abusers can be
extremely manipulative. They can play-act in astounding
ways. Abusers have come up with many and varied ruses to
obtain access to their partners and to get them back home.
The church is not immune to such manipulation. Again,
there must be a careful balance between acceptance and
trust of the abuser and protection of the victim. As in all
areas of Christian ministry, discernment and wisdom
should be sought from the Holy Spirit. A healthy scepticism
is often better than simple naivety in such circumstances.
However, people do change; indeed that is the whole
message of the gospel. In this case, however, it is for Karen
to make the final decisions about John's genuineness and
her own safety.

It is important to remember that each case is different. A
family, no matter how 'dysfunctional', is comprised of
individuals who have their own characteristics, their own
ways of coping with stress and hurt and who must make
their own decisions about life. There is no formula by which
all violent families can be 'treated'. There is no easy five-
step plan for victims to achieve a non-violent relationship
or a new life. There are, however, a wide range of options
and services open to victims, although their availability
may vary from area to area. This chapter has given a
practical introduction to the types of needs a victim may
typically have and the nature of the remedies available. The
following two chapters examine the traditional philosophy
behind such service provision and suggest a more ideal
situation of the emphasis being on eradication of the
violence rather than escape of the victim.

Seven

Escape – The Traditional Response

In 1971, Erin Pizzey founded Chiswick Women's Aid, the first refuge facility for abused women in the country. Although this facility was a vital, practical contribution in terms of service provision for victims, its significance was far greater. Its establishment was a public statement, saying in no uncertain terms that measures needed to be taken to deal with the socially unacceptable phenomenon of domestic violence. That statement led to the growing recognition of wife abuse in England and other countries and proved to be the catalyst for much of the legislative and social service provision which was developed to protect and assist victims over the following years.

The focus of all the provisions which ensued has been on facilitating the victim's escape from the violent situation. The emphasis has been on getting the victim and her children away from the threat of immediate violence and to help her re-establish a life elsewhere. Generally the law has placed the issue of domestic violence into the so-called 'private arena'. It has categorized domestic violence as a family problem rather than a social one and has emphasized the use of the civil law rather than the criminal. Few attempts have been made, until recently, to address the root causes of the problem. This situation is significant because a focus on escape from the problem does not necessarily serve a victim's best interests.

The civil law

Chapter 6 dealt with the current law on injunctions which is undoubtedly an improvement on the previous situation. Originally one could not apply for a protective order unless there was a case already before the court –for example, suing an abuser for damages for assault or trespass. It is only very recently that a victim could sue for harassment alone without violence. An alternative for married couples was to petition for divorce.

The situation did improve dramatically with the Domestic Violence and Matrimonial Proceedings Act 1976 which enabled an injunction application to be brought as a free-standing case by married couples and by cohabitees who were still living together at the time of the last incident. It was under this Act that the concept of molestation explained in chapter 5 was really developed. The Act allowed for both non-molestation orders and ouster injunctions – orders excluding an abuser from a house, part of it, or from an area in which the house was located. These applications were made in either the county court or the High Court.

Further, but more restricted remedies, were introduced by the Domestic Proceedings and Magistrates Court Act 1978 which, as its name suggests, enabled personal protection orders to be obtained, by spouses only (not cohabitees), in the Magistrates Court.

At first glance, then, one might think that the civil law has, since the mid-seventies, been offering victims a good range of protection. However, a more critical look at the law reveals inadequacies. In fact, a senior judge in the case of Davis v Johnson[1] described the civil law as offering 'a miserable mouse of protection'. Indeed, Erin Pizzey, giving

---

[1] [1979] A.C. 264

evidence to a Select Committee on Violence in Marriage once said, 'The pot of black pepper I have in my handbag is of greater protection to me than a High Court injunction.' The Family Law Act 1996 increases protection and availability of orders in two ways. Firstly, it widens the list of persons against whom applications for injunctions can be made on a free-standing basis. Now there is a whole list of 'associated persons' against whom applications can be made, while previously it was limited to spouses and cohabitees. Secondly, the Act has made Powers of Arrest easier to obtain than they were previously. However, there are still problems with the civil law as it stands when the issues of domestic violence are looked at from an overall perspective.

To begin with, many injunction applications are heard in 'chambers'. That is, the case is heard in a closed court to which the public are refused entry. Some would say that the closed court is in a victim's interest in that she has to recount the painful details of assaults to only a limited number of people. It also prevents the abuser from bringing in family and friends to make the experience even more difficult for the victim. On the other hand, some would say that the system works to the victim's disadvantage. Firstly, the closed court communicates that the violence is a 'family problem'. It individualizes the issue and makes it look as if this family is unusually dysfunctional. Domestic violence cases are thus put in the same category as cases where children are to be taken into care or where adults cannot agree how to split their assets in a divorce. Thus, attention is drawn away from the societal nature of the problem and the way in which cultural values support the violence. The problem is portrayed solely as a dispute between two adults and society's interest in the violence is denied. Secondly, the issue is characterized as 'private' and as something which should remain beyond the public's gaze. In giving the victims privacy in court, the system is saying that domestic violence is no-one else's concern. This message has important implications in shaping responses to domestic violence, as we shall see later.

The current legislation reflects the fact that no attention

was paid to the root causes of domestic violence. Consequently, no attempt is made in the civil law as it stands to address those causes and prevent the reoccurrence of the violence. Before 1976 injunctions were often obtained, ancillary to divorce, where the clear emphasis was on escape from the situation. Right up until the introduction of the Family Law Act 1996, victims who were not married to or cohabiting with their abusers had to sue for damages and obtain an injunction attached to such an application. This legislation gave the message that protection was not the primary concern of the court's jurisdiction. Nor does it acknowledge the additional trauma and difficulties suffered by a woman who is assaulted within what is supposed to be an intimate and stable relationship.

The current domestic violence legislation is still stunted in its effectiveness by the principles it has inherited from its background. Court proceedings are still adversarial, pitting one adult against the other. There is no agency which will take on the responsibility of obtaining and keeping in effect a court order on a victim's behalf. In the criminal system, however, once a victim presses charges the Crown Prosecution Service takes over the burden of conducting the court case. Taking civil law proceedings can demand a lot of the victim's time and energy, at a time when she is feeling at her most vulnerable. The following example of an injunction case, which went as far as enforcement action, illustrates well just how much responsibility and effort is required from the victim. The case is not unusual save that the victim here perhaps showed more resilience than other victims and was able to see her case through to the bitter end.

Sandra was married to Bill, who was violent and verbally abusive to her on a regular basis. They had two small children and lived in their own home. Sandra came to see me after the violence had put her in hospital for a broken jaw. She rang to make an appointment with me and I asked her to come into the office as soon as she could. She then had to arrange for a babysitter and an 'alibi' so that her husband would not suspect that she was seeking legal advice. She was afraid that if he found out he would hospitalize her again. She managed to come in that same afternoon.

She then had to tell me all her problems. I needed to know the details of past violence, as well as about the most recent incidents and about her accommodation and children. I also needed to know about her financial position so that we could assess whether she was eligible for legal aid or not. She had a small part-time job which meant that a long legal aid form had to be filled in which asked detailed questions about her finances. (Had she been on income support the form would have been much shorter.) She found it very emotionally difficult telling all these details to a stranger and was worried about her children being alone. However, she did want to know all her rights and exactly what her options were. I, therefore, gave her lengthy advice – about divorce or separation, about her entitlement to welfare benefits and to the assets of the marriage and, of course, about the way she could protect herself from the violence. Not surprisingly, she found all this a lot to comprehend at one time.

She decided that she needed urgent protection from her husband and that we could consider more long-term issues at a later stage. We therefore filled in legal aid forms and I gave her information about her local Women's Aid Centre which ran an emergency refuge. However, she decided to stay at her sister's house that night.

When she had gone I finished the legal aid application and was able to get the legal aid granted within half an hour or so, since my firm had a Legal Aid Franchise, allowing us to issue emergency legal aid in-house. This meant that, with the help of a good secretary, I was able to have all the court papers prepared by noon the next day. I rang Sandra at her sister's house in the morning to let her know that she could go to court that afternoon. She was both pleased and shocked. She was adamant that she needed protection but also felt that matters were moving very fast. The children had been distressed at not going home the previous night and she had had very little sleep. Nevertheless, she decided she still wanted to go ahead with the case.

We met at the court at two o'clock. She had to read through her affidavit, a statement of the facts on which her application was based, which she then had to swear was true. She found it shocking to see her problems written down in black and white and was worried about her husband's reaction when he eventually saw the papers. Again, she was given the choice of not carrying on but chose to go ahead. She was very nervous about going into a court room as it was a new experience for her and was worried that she might get emotional in front of a judge or that he would be harsh with her. Whilst we were waiting, I tried to reassure her as much as possible. When we went in before a District Judge, he granted an order that her husband should not be violent or abusive to her. We had asked that her husband be ordered to leave the house so that Sandra could return with the children. This part of the application was adjourned to the next hearing, as is common, to give Bill a chance to get legal representation.

Sandra went back to her sister's house with the children, and I arranged for the injunction and all the application papers to be served on Bill by a private detective. The next hearing was to be in five days time, on the following Monday.

Sandra met me at court again on the Monday. Unfortunately, the private detective could not find Bill. This meant that he still did not know about the court case. It also meant that he had not been served with the injunction and so it was not effective. Sandra was still unprotected, a fact which she found hard to accept. A court will not make a long-term order against someone who does not know about the case and has not had a chance to put his side of the story across. So, another order was made that Bill should not be violent to Sandra and a new hearing date was set for a weeks time.

Sandra then had to make a decision. Either she stayed with her sister, where she felt in the way and where the children were fretting, or else she returned to the house. She felt that by 'disappearing' for awhile she had inevitably antagonized Bill and would be assaulted as soon as he saw her. She again considered moving into a refuge, but decided to stay with her sister. At this stage she also had to go to the benefits agency to claim welfare benefits as she had no money to live on. She had to fill in more forms and explain about the violence yet again.

In the middle of that week she received some letters from the Legal Aid Board. These were standard letters but they were very formal and she did not really understand them. She therefore rang me to be reassured that they were nothing to worry about. I then heard that Bill had been served with the papers and so I rang her to let her know that the next hearing could go ahead.

At the third hearing Bill came to court. Sandra was very worried about being near him or meeting him by accident in the street, so she came to my offices first and we travelled to court together, arriving early and securing a side room for privacy. Bill had taken initial legal advice, but, because he was working and would not get legal aid, he represented himself. I asked him to give undertakings – to promise to leave the house – but he refused to do so. A full hearing was therefore necessary.

Sandra had to sit across a table from Bill, who was behaving in a most reasonable way. She had to answer a few questions asked by me, and then the judge told Bill he could ask her questions. Usually this questioning is done by a lawyer but, as Bill was alone, there was no cushion between Sandra and Bill. He was actually careful to be reasonable in his questions, but he asked Sandra why she was lying and why she was doing this when it was all an exaggeration. He accused her of doing it to make sure she got the house if they divorced and suggested her true motivation might be that she had another man. This was traumatic for Sandra, even though the questions never transgressed what was reasonable for Bill to ask to put his defence across. Bill then gave evidence and Sandra could not help but cry at what she later described as 'unbelievable lies'.

Fortunately, after the judge had heard both sides he believed Sandra implicitly and ordered that Bill should not be abusive or violent to her and that he should leave the house within forty-eight hours. Three days later, Sandra took the children back to the house. She had only been there a few hours when Bill came around, saying that he had forgotten his shaver. She threw it down out of the window to him, but he then began to be verbally abusive to her, shouting in the street. She had to decide whether or not to call the police. The children, who did not understand the situation, were begging her to let Daddy in. Eventually a neighbour came out to complain about the noise and so Bill left voluntarily.

However, over the next three days he returned on four occasions, each time on the pretext of wanting to see the children or to collect belongings. I communicated with him directly, suggesting that his niece collect the children at set times for him to see them and that he give us one list of his belongings which we would then deliver to him. This meant that he had no reason to keep going to the house. It resulted in peace for a couple of weeks.

However, one Saturday night he came around drunk, forced his way into the house and assaulted her again. She had no alternative but to call the police who arrested him but released him the next morning, when he parked his car outside the house and sat there for hours on end watching the house.

On the Monday she phoned me in a state of great anxiety. She was concerned that there was nothing she could do since she did not phone the police the first time and because he was only sitting outside. I explained to her that, if she wanted to, she could apply to have him committed to prison for breaching the court order. She agonized about this decision for a day or so. Her concern was that the children would miss their father if he was sent to prison. Then he began to cause trouble again and she felt that she had no alternative.

I applied to have her legal aid amended to cover a committal application and prepared her new affidavit. She had to arrange another babysitter so that she could come into the office again to swear it and we posted the papers off to the court asking for a hearing date as soon as possible.

The hearing was listed in a few days time. Unfortunately it clashed with another big case which I was doing and which I had to attend. I therefore briefed a barrister to represent Sandra and asked one of my junior colleagues to go to court with her. This is a common practice; indeed, many solicitors do not do their own advocacy in court at any stage of the proceedings. It was unavoidable. However, it did mean that Sandra had to meet two new strangers and confide in them on the very day she was applying to send her own husband to prison.

That day at court the lists were very busy and, although she had been told to be at court at half past ten, it was not until three o'clock that her case was heard, by which time she was very nervous indeed. Bill had been at court all the time and so she had been afraid even to go to the toilet alone whilst waiting. The judge listened to Bill, who was very contrite. He apologized to the court and the judge gave him a suspended sentence of six weeks. Sandra was in two minds about this result. On the one hand, Bill was still free and might come to the house again. On the other, she did not have to struggle with the task of telling the children that he was in prison.

Fortunately, the threat of this suspended sentence was enough to make Bill realize the error of his ways and the violence and harassment ceased. Had it not, Sandra would have had to make yet another visit to court. As it was, Bill decided to issue divorce proceedings against her, which she found hard to bear. He was very awkward throughout the divorce process and, whilst Sandra got a good settlement in the end, she had months of unnecessarily protracted legal proceedings to endure before it all ended.

This story shows just how many decisions and court hearings a woman may have to endure. Of course other cases are more straightforward, but Sandra's case is by no means unusual.

We have already seen how abused women frequently suffer severe psychological problems, loss of confidence, inability to cope with officialdom and so on. Also, women may be afraid to act at any one of those stages, simply for fear of retribution. Thus, placing the responsibility on victims to avail themselves of these remedies may in itself render them unavailable to many victims. We will see in chapter 9 how the church may help alleviate these problems.

Also, the remedies for stopping the violence are short-term. Three months was the standard length of an order before the Family Law Act 1996, which does allow a longer period. However, it still remains at the court's discretion whether to give an order for the maximum time allowed or not. The Act is very new, but it may be that three months will remain the standard with longer orders being granted for exceptional cases. The orders merely forbid the abusive behaviour and threaten a sanction for breach of the order. They do not identify and address the causes of the behaviour in order to prevent reoffending. Rather, the emphasis is on minimal intervention, especially in applications asking for an abuser to be removed from a property. The assumption is that the orders will give protection for long enough for the parties to separate and to establish separate lives, or that a 'short, sharp shock' will effect a change of behaviour in the abuser to allow the parties to continue to live together. Orders are not intended to begin the long process of work with the abuser and his family to get rid of the violence.

The criminal law

This theme of minimal intervention in domestic violence cases has traditionally been reflected in the criminal law also. The last few years have, admittedly, seen a sudden issuing of police force policies on domestic violence by the police. There has been a corresponding increase in police recording of domestic assaults and an improvement in the way that the police respond to domestic violence. However, the legacy of the traditional attitude still remains, particularly in officers with some length of service who have not taken on board the new changes – either because of personal reluctance to do so, because the new attitudes have not yet filtered down through the ranks, or because training has not yet been provided to all officers.

The criminal laws of assault apply equally to husbands and wives as to strangers. However, traditionally, the police have been reluctant to intervene in so-called 'domestics'. Historically they have been warned against such intervention. The Bristol City Police Instruction Book of 1880, for example, stated, 'The Police are not to interfere unnecessarily between a man and his wife unless it is absolutely necessary to prevent serious violence to either party or public disturbance.'

From such guidelines, policing scholars argue that an ideological caution developed in which it was ingrained in police to keep out of family matters as much as they could. It is also argued that this attitude is reinforced by years of experience. Police have found the law powerless to stop repeated domestic violence incidents. They have found themselves returning to the same families over and over again and have developed the attitude that intervention is a waste of time. Further, the police have specifically justified non-intervention by reference to the specific familial nature of the abuse. A (quasi-) marital relationship has been seen as private and self-regulating. Borkowski says,

> The statutory powers of the Police . . . to intervene and seek information can also be viewed by outsiders as part of the armoury available to outsiders to breach and control partnership boundaries.[2]

In other words, in today's society we are very conscious of civil rights and issues regarding an individual's privacy. The danger with domestic violence is that the abuser's right to privacy in the family is given a higher priority than the victim's conflicting right to protection.

Susan Edwards, in her book *Policing Domestic Violence*, argues that this policy of non-intervention arose, not only as a result of such theoretical beliefs about family privacy, but also indirectly from police operational practice. She suggests that political events like the inner-city riots of 1980 and 1981, the miners strike, poll tax demonstrations and football hooliganism has led to an emphasis on public order policing. This emphasis exists, she says, both at the governmental level and at the 'sharp-end' of policing. Putting an emphasis on public order policing, she says, corresponds to the consequential marginalization of private or 'domestic' crime.[3]

When the policing of domestic violence has been compared with these other, more high-profile, more demanding and more exciting public order duties, police in the past have commonly described domestic violence as being a 'waste of time'. There has been a common feeling that their response was ineffective or unwanted. One officer commented to a researcher, 'You get a piggy in the middle

---

[2] Borkowski, M., *Marital Violence – the Community Response* (1983)
[3] Edwards, S.M., *Policing Domestic Violence* (London: Sage Publications 1989)

feeling sometimes. You get let in but none of the parties are pleased to see you.'[4]

There is a common view among police that women frequently drop charges before court cases and so, rather than spending time on paperwork, police have often told women that there was nothing they could do for her and that she should go to court and get an injunction through a solicitor. In the past, little value has been placed on domestic violence work in terms of promotion, and so there has been little incentive for individual officers to challenge common perceptions.

All this may seem to be an unfair attack on the police. Indeed, forces are now increasingly providing limited but specialized domestic violence services, which were looked at in chapter 6 on service provision. It is fair to say, however, that many of the police's problems stem from the nature of the criminal law itself. Women do drop charges with alarming frequency. Why is this? Often they are from a community which discourages collaboration with the police and so, whilst they will call the police for emergency protection, they are reluctant to press matters any further. However, we must also consider what victims would profit from pressing charges. What incentive is there to do so? Often domestic assaults are still knocked down by prosecutors to lower offences to ensure a 'result' at court. Sentences tend to be light for minor assault offences, often meaning that the abuser remains free, even if on a community sentence such as probation. The abuser who is locked up may just return after he has spent his time in prison, still violent but even more angry. A fine will simply deplete the victim's own family finances.

The point is, again, that with the exception of some probation schemes, as mentioned in chapter 6 on service provision, the criminal law does not look at the causes of domestic violence either. The emphasis is instead on punishment, not reform, except in the sense that some believe that punishment itself engenders reform. However,

---

[4] Bourlet, A., *Police Intervention in Marital Violence* (Buckingham: Open University Press 1990)

the individual cases in which the criminal justice system makes a specific attempt to address the causes of domestic violence are few and far between. There is benefit in using the criminal law to declare domestic violence a publicly unacceptable offence. However, individual victims are often not served well by the system.

The effect of all this is that victims are thrown back on the civil system, with all its drawbacks mentioned above. Alternatively, victims avoid the law entirely and simply leave the abusive relationship by taking advantage of refuges or rehousing laws. The emphasis is then, again, on escaping from the violence.

Why is this emphasis on escape of concern? From a Christian point of view, this system facilitates and encourages family breakdown, which is something that grieves God. Escape also gives rise to other problems, such as single-parent families and poverty, which the Bible makes clear are not ideal conditions. From a practical viewpoint, emphasizing escape is not the most efficient way to deal with domestic violence. Financially, it means the state often has to support two family units. More importantly, it does nothing to stop reoccurrence of the violence. Victims who try to escape but are unable to do so may make repeated demands on the system, seeking further injunctions or moving in and out of refuges. When a victim does escape, the abuser often moves on to a new abusive relationship, and the pattern repeats itself. The victim is left with all her vulnerabilities and hurts intact. She may have escaped the violence but will not really have escaped its effects. Many victims even go on to enter a second abusive relationship. None of this really gives protection to the victim. In order to give true, effective, deep-rooted, long-lasting protection, the emphasis must be changed. Rather than facilitating escape from abuse, the focus should be on eradicating the violence altogether.

Eight

Emphasizing Eradication

'I want to help but I just don't know where to start', is a common plea which applies as much to domestic violence as it does to famine, child neglect or any other social problem with which the church might become involved. Once a person realizes that a friend or relative is suffering from domestic violence, it is natural to want to help them. Also, it is hoped that church members who have read the earlier chapters of this book will have learned enough about domestic violence to want to become involved at a wider, social level, as well as assisting individuals in their social circle who may be victims.

But where to start? Can more harm than good be done by well-meaning but misplaced intentions? Might intervening in a delicate family situation make matters worse? Shouldn't such social issues be left to the professionals? Certainly, it is always highly advisable for helpers to gain as much knowledge and training as possible. In some areas, such as counselling, it is important to have professional qualifications in order to give the best service. But the church can still make a valuable contribution. Chapter 9 will give a whole range of practical suggestions on how the church, and its members, can help victims deal with their own problems and how the church can play a part in eradicating domestic violence from society.

First, however, let us consider the theoretic basis on which such help should be given. The most effective help in any situation is always given with clear aims and a clear understanding about what is to be achieved. A muddled and unclear attempt at intervention can result in differing messages being given to a victim, causing confusion and distress. Without a coordinated approach to practical assistance, the left hand may even be undoing what the right hand is trying to accomplish. This chapter, therefore, will look at what the church should be trying to achieve and why.

In previous chapters we have established that domestic violence is a social problem with deep roots in the cultural values on which our society is based. The last chapter outlined the shortcomings of a system based solely on helping victims to escape from violence. Of course, the only solution for some families is escape – either on a short-term basis, as emergency crisis provision, or alternatively on a long-term basis where no other solution appears available or workable. However, escape should only be one of the range of weapons used against domestic violence and should not be the main aim of helpers. It has also been argued that leaving victims to enjoy 'family privacy' does not help them. All the suggestions presented from now on, therefore, assume that the church will adopt an active policy of intervention. The question is: what approach should the church adopt when deciding to intervene?

Approaches to intervention

Intervention in domestic violence cases can be either compassion-based or control-based.

A compassion-based approach emphasizes the compassion shown to the abuser. In such an approach he is seen as a kind of victim himself – a victim of his poor family background, a victim of inherent personality traits, or a victim of the cultural norms which have encouraged and condoned his behaviour. The emphasis is on looking at societal and developmental causes for his behaviour. A programme which adopts such a compassionate approach would typically try to support the whole family unit, not just the victim, and would want to work with the abuser, affording him compassion and kindness. It would, of course, be essentially non-punitive. It would focus on helping the abuser overcome his 'violence problems' and improve his family life by developing more appropriate ways to deal with interpersonal relationships. The violence is thus seen as being damaging to the abuser as well as to the victim.

A control-based approach, on the other hand, would be much more punitive. Full responsibility would be placed on the abuser for his actions. He would be seen as 'in the wrong' and needing correction and punishment for his deliberate misdemeanours. There would be much less emphasis on support for the abuser – such support being given instead to the victim, who would be seen as the one in need. A control-based approach would lay a heavy emphasis on separation of the parties and on legal sanctions, both to limit the abuser's behaviour and to remove the victim from the danger caused wilfully by the abuser.

In fact, for the church to choose just one of these approaches would probably mean oversimplifying the issues involved. If we refer back to the combined causation model developed in chapter 4, it becomes clear that a combination of the above two approaches, which are not necessarily mutually exclusive, is the most appropriate way forward. For the model, whilst recognizing the operation of cultural norms and values on family dynamics, does not deny that abusers are responsible for their own violent actions. Violence may be legitimized in society, but abusers nevertheless do not have to use violence. Violence may even be a learned behaviour, but it is an illegal one, and it is the abuser's responsibility to learn alternative behaviour patterns.

So, when a church is considering what measures it would like to take to deal with domestic violence, its response should be partly control-based. The church needs to emphasize that domestic violence is not just unfortunate; it is unacceptable. The church needs to be clear that abusers are not automatons at the mercy of the society around them, but are sensible human beings responsible for their actions. However, the church's aim should also be to maintain *healthy* family units. It is not suggested that families suffering from violence should be kept together for the sake of it or that suffering should be perpetuated for the sake of academic principle – that is, a biblical mandate against divorce. Rather, it is the role of the church to bring the Christian message of healing and reconciliation to families in a very real and practical sense as well as in a spiritual sense. To communicate that message, an element of a control-based response is also needed. The church should provide abusers with firm guidelines and support, conducive to their accepting a new non-violent set of attitudes and learning new ways of relating to their partners.

Orientations of intervention

Such a combination of compassion and control, however, only provides a basic framework. It is also necessary to consider in which direction such intervention is to be channelled. Just who is to be the subject of the church's aid? As Figure 9 shows, there are three main areas in which a church could channel its energies. Intervention can be victim-orientated, offender-orientated or society-orientated. All three orientations are necessary if domestic violence is to be eradicated. Of course, a church may have only limited time and resources and may want to focus on one type of intervention in its practical programmes, perhaps after checking what is already available to victims in their locality. However, all three strands are equally important.

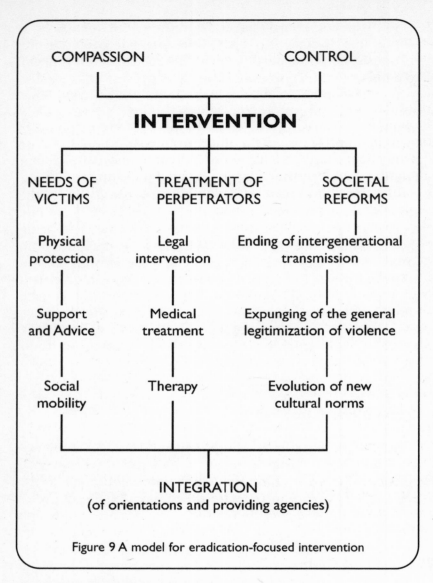

Figure 9 A model for eradication-focused intervention

1. Victim-orientated intervention

That intervention should be focused on the needs of victims perhaps seems obvious. However, if a church is to take a broad view of domestic violence then it is useful to remember that the needs of the victims should really remain central. If a church is running a programme for abusers, it is easy to become sidetracked and focus solely on their needs. A careful eye needs to be kept on the needs of individual victims and of victims in general. In assessing the value and success of any programme of intervention, the following questions must be asked: Is the programme helping victims? Will it make their lives free from violence or will it simply cause them other problems?

One client sought advice about a divorce just over a year after she had pressed charges against her husband for assault. He had been prosecuted, found guilty and sentenced to a period of probation. It was a condition of that probation that he attend a domestic violence course run by the probation service. Intrigued as to how she viewed the effect of this course on her relationship with her husband, I asked her how the course had benefited them. She replied that her husband had stopped the use of physical violence but was still intimidating towards her. More interestingly, she said that she felt the course had given him the attention he loved. She felt that she was still affected by the previous violence, still unable to trust him and still had a very low self-worth. That particular lady, unfortunately, had been unable to attend the support group run by the probation service for the partners of abusers on the course. Nor had she ever been referred to other agencies such as Women's Aid which may have been able to help her. The story illustrates well that the victims need attention and that their overall needs should be considered in depth; the focus should be wider than simply the cessation of physical violence.

Victims' needs are wide-ranging. They can include:

Physical protection

- legal court orders
- emergency help from the police
- emergency accommodation
- rehousing in a secure place

■ assistance in dealing with arrangements for an abuser's contact with the children to ensure no further abuse

Support and advice

■ treatment for physical injuries

■ help with emotional and psychological damage

■ help dealing with agencies such as the police, solicitors, housing departments, etc.

■ information about their legal rights and entitlements

Greater social mobility

■ access to jobs at realistic wages

■ competent childcare for working mothers

■ an end to sexual discrimination and condemnation for having been abused

Of course, the church will also be concerned with a victim's spiritual and emotional needs. These may include a need to experience true love, to recover from the hurtful criticisms made by an abuser which have resulted in a negative self-image, the need to learn to trust again, and so forth.

2. Offender-orientated intervention

It is in the victim's interest for any intervention to also consider the offender. Given that he is the source of the violence, it makes sense that the best protection and help which can be given to a victim would include helping an abuser address the reasons for his behaviour and giving him assistance and encouragement (and, if necessary, motivation through unpleasant sanctions) for changing his behaviour.

This consideration of the offender can be done through

the legal system. Obviously the church may only be indirectly involved in the use of the law, but church helpers can play an important part in making the system more accessible – or at the least endurable – for victims to use. The church can also lobby for changes in the law which would give a better deal to victims. A church member's instinct may be to try and steer a family away from the legal system and to try and help them resolve their differences by negotiation alone. Any family lawyer worth their salt would agree that in the majority of family cases, the more that can be done by agreement and conciliation, the better. In this way disputes can be resolved more quickly and with the least bitterness and distress to the parties. However, in the case of domestic violence, there are good arguments why the legal system should be invoked.

Law enforcement officers, be they police officers or judges, represent the authority of the state in a way that other helpers – counsellors, social workers or mediators for example – do not. Thus the involvement of the legal system sends the important message to the abuser that domestic violence is a serious offence and one which the public cares about and will not condone. The laws in different countries do vary, although in practice there is generally a core body of law which is similar in all states. The law of any given country is in effect a statement, issued via a democratic process, of what is unacceptable behaviour to the majority in that society. The law, then, is essentially an agent of social control and carries with it the power to allocate responsibility and to express clear condemnation of those who transgress its precepts.

Also, when working with victims of domestic violence, it is important not to underestimate possible danger. Women are frequently killed as a result of domestic violence. Whilst it may well be appropriate to work with both the abuser and the victim to try and remove the violence from the relationship, there should be no hesitation in seeking to protect a vulnerable victim in the meantime. Civil court applications for injunctions can be resolved by way of undertakings, if possible, to reduce the nastiness of the proceedings. However, if an injunction or undertaking is in place, an abuser knows that the violence is to stop and the victim has some protection, together with the option of enforcing the order if the work with the family is not successful. This order also has the effect of giving an abuser a powerful message: if he agrees to take part in therapeutic work he is not being generous or enlightened, nor is he to be praised for agreeing to 'humour' his partner. Rather, he is labelled from the beginning as dangerous, and his behaviour is branded as unacceptable.

The law can also increase the cost of the violence for offenders. The model of combined causation discussed in chapter 4 is not indestructible. There are various points in the model which are natural break points – places where the pressure of change can break the cycle of domestic violence being caused, reinforced and then repeated. These break points are discussed in more detail in chapter 9 and are also illustrated there in diagrammatic form. One such break point is at the stage of reinforcement, where the increased costs of violence can play an important part.

The law can make domestic violence less 'functional' – less 'profitable' – for abusers. The criminal law can impose a range of sentences from fines and probation orders or other community sentences through to terms of imprisonment. The civil law can require a man to leave his home and, if an order is enforced, can also impose fines or imprisonment. Just having legal proceedings taken against him can increase the costs of violence to an abuser, causing inconvenience and perhaps embarrassment. It makes him stand out and makes him vulnerable – to inconvenience at the very least, and potentially to the loss of liberty. The law may not be perfect, but even as a blunt tool it can do a job.

The same can apply to law in the informal sense, as in a set of rules or by-laws of a club or group – or the church. Abusers can be church members. Church leaders wanting to take domestic violence seriously should consider the powers within membership rules to impose sanctions on members who are violent. Should abusers be allowed to retain membership? Should membership be suspended, to be reinstated in the future if certain conditions are met? Should abusers be prevented from undertaking formal leadership roles within the church or even from helping with less formal jobs and activities? Ostracism is a strong term, and certainly the aim of a church leader should not be to humiliate or to turn away an abuser. However, there is a place within the church for loving discipline. Use of the 'church laws' in this sense can have the same effects as the formal legal system. It will increase the cost by causing shame and by making an abuser's behaviour public. It will also clearly condemn domestic violence as unacceptable – to God and to the church.

Secondly, in an offender-orientated approach, medical treatment may in some cases be appropriate. A regression to a completely psychiatric model, in which all domestic violence is blamed on an individual's sickness, whether of mind or of body, is to be avoided. However, it is appropriate to recognize the need for treatment in those cases where violence may be attributable, in whole or in part, to an organic, psychiatric, environmental or nutritional source. Some people would distinguish violence arising from medical conditions such as neurological disorders or head injuries from 'domestic violence' proper. Given that churches dealing with such people will still be faced with victims in need, however, such distinctions do not seem particularly helpful here. Medical treatment may also be needed where domestic violence is linked with drug or alcohol abuse or addiction. Of course, offenders undergoing medical treatment may still need to unlearn what may have become instinctive behaviours. As with other forms of intervention, medical treatment is not a single magic cure but one of a range of options in an approach which will fully meet a family's needs.

The third approach in an offender-orientated view of domestic violence is therapy for the offender. This is perhaps an area where the church might like to become involved. It is, therefore, useful to look at the types of therapy which experts have developed so that a church can assess its own capabilities and limitations and decide just how much it can effectively offer to abusers. Therapy can take many forms. One expert, Roy, points out that there are dangers in oversimplification: treating all abusers with the same strategy is unlikely to achieve the same result. She claims the key term is 'differential diagnosis'. Thus programmes developed for abusers tend to use different methods, and a local church may wish to become familiar with local programmes for referral purposes. However, the following two main types of programmes can be identified.

Therapy combined with medical treatment

The first main group of programmes combines therapy with medical diagnosis, much as a drug programme may deal with the physical dependency and side effects of, say, crack cocaine, whilst also addressing lifestyle issues and the addict's psychological dependency. A prime example of such a programme is one which was developed at the East Orange, New Jersey, Veteran's Administration Hospital in the United States. They developed a three-pronged approach, with treatment strategies specific to each category.

The first category of patient included those whose violent behaviour could be attributed to psychiatric conditions: epilepsy, tumours, paranoid schizophrenia, pathological jealousy and toxic states caused by drug or alcohol misuse. Treatment of these conditions focused on drug use, neurological treatment and / or treatment of the addiction to the toxic substances.

The second category of patients encompassed those whose violence may have had an organic, physical origin but where the main factor was psychodynamic. Abusers falling into this category were treated with individual psychotherapy.

The third category was classed specifically as 'Domestic Violence'. This type of violence was acknowledged to stem from many causes, although the people running this particular programme believed that domestic violence was due to a breakdown in social stability and corresponding levels of stress – either external stress, caused by social and environmental factors, or internal stress, attributable to the abuser's own nature. Family violence which did not fall into the first two categories was then dealt with in family, marital or group therapy for both victims and offenders, as was thought appropriate.[1]

The point of describing such a programme in a book of this nature is not, of course, to suggest that a church should be making similar provisions – it is to make the point that some violence cannot be treated within the church and other specialist help will be needed. The church may well have an additional role to play with that family whilst medical treatment is given, but it should not attempt to shoulder the whole burden in inappropriate cases.

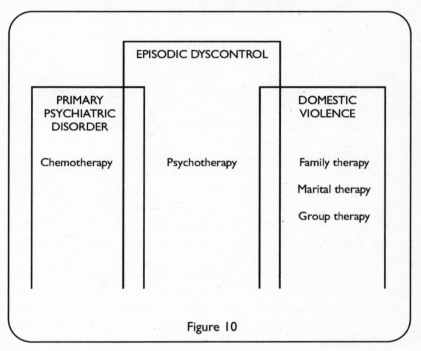

Figure 10

Counselling as therapy

The second main form of therapy does not involve medical or psychiatric diagnosis but aims to change the attitudes of the abuser. There are now many excellent texts which deal with both secular and pastoral counselling.

---

[1] Taken from Roy, M., *The Abusive Partner. An Analysis of Domestic Battering* (Van Nostrand Reinhold Co. 1982)

Indeed, counselling has now developed beyond a 'listening ear' offered by a well-meaning Christian into a much more regulated and professionalized sphere of ministry. The Association of Christian Counsellors now exists to coordinate those offering Christian counselling.

Such Christian counselling may emphasize theological teaching or may borrow more heavily from the wide variety of secular approaches – from behaviouralism, psychoanalysis, and so on. Techniques may also vary: such terms as 'cognitive processing' or 'neuro-linguistic counselling' will be familiar to specialists in the subject. Counselling may take place with the victim and / or abuser individually or with the couple together – or even a combination of the two.

It is beyond the scope of this book to enter into a lengthy discussion about the merits of any given approach to counselling. Two points, however, will be useful here. Firstly, counselling is very different to befriending and does involve specialist skills which need to be learned. If a victim is to be offered formal counselling, then the counsellor should have had training in counselling generally, as well as, arguably, in the issues surrounding domestic violence itself. The second point is that to be successful, whatever techniques or theoretical approaches are adopted, the counselling must start from the premise that domestic violence is wrong and unacceptable and that, whilst society may play a part in condoning violence, the abuser is ultimately responsible for his actions.

Counselling which simply looks at the causes of the violence will not challenge the outworking of those causes and so will not stop the violence. Allowing an abuser to acknowledge that he beats his wife because he grew up seeing his own father do the same does not really take the couple any further. Similarly, counselling which goes no further than stress or anger management may not ever get to the root of the problem. If Bill is violent to his wife because he feels that he should have absolute control over her, then getting him to stop hitting her will be only half the answer. He will still feel that he should be in control and will find other ways of obtaining that control. The violence may stop, but other forms of abuse are likely to continue. We have already seen that such 'masked violence' or emotional abuse can be just as harmful as physical beatings. To be useful, the counselling must be offender-orientated. For to stop the violence may benefit the victim but it does not meet all the needs of the offender or change his tendencies at root level. The focus must not just be on the *violence* but on the *violent offender.*

3. Society-orientated intervention

The whole premise of this book is that domestic violence is embedded in our society as a product of the values which we, as a community, hold. It follows, then, that the third orientation of intervention should be towards society as a whole. The intervention, to have its widest possible effect, must look at the root causes of domestic violence and the ways in which it has become established in society. Gelles summed up the rationale behind society-orientated intervention well when he wrote:

> If, as we argue, the widespread incidence and severity of family violence is a product of cultural norms which tolerate and approve of violence and the particular social organisation of the family, then the ultimate solutions and the most effective programmes of primary intervention will have to realise that no meaningful change can occur until something is done to change prevailing norms and other social organisation of the family.[2]

As the model for eradication-focused intervention shows, there are three general groups of societal reform for the church to consider. The first question is: what can be done to end the reinforcement and intergenerational transmission of the violence? If this question is not considered when a programme for intervention is considered, then the work will never be done – each generation will present exactly the same problems. Essentially, the aim of those working to eradicate domestic violence should be to do themselves out of a job by

---

[2] Gelles, R.J., *Family Violence* (1979) p.20

preventing the next generation inheriting the legacy of domestic violence. The combined causation model diagram has made it clear how fundamental the legitimization of violence in our society is to the perpetuation of domestic violence. So, secondly, there must be an attempt to expunge this legitimization. Then, once that has been done, new cultural norms need to evolve. It does no good to remove the bad and leave a vacuum that will soon be filled again with the bad. It is no use telling people how not to behave and how not to think but not giving them a positive alternative. It is perhaps here that the church comes into its own. A congregation can often offer victims and abusers a whole range of practical provisions to alleviate their situations. If it wishes, the church can become involved in political and moral debate and media campaigns to try and halt the violence. However, the church is not alone in being able to do those things. There are increasing numbers of service providers who will take on all or some of these tasks. This, of course, does not mean that there is no room for the church to make this kind of contribution. Far from it. Indeed, the final chapter gives a whole range of suggestions for concrete practical projects which the church may wish to undertake.

However, the church does have one clear advantage over other social agencies. It is the guardian of the Word of God, the ultimate blueprint for life. Other agencies will have worthy pieces of advice and experience to impart to victims and, in their level of experience about the specific issues of domestic violence, may well have more knowledge than the church. However, unless their teaching stems from the Word of God, it will never be complete. If the fundamental root of domestic violence lies in sin, then the ultimate solution lies in salvation and renewal through the working of the Holy Spirit. It is this message which the church can, and indeed should, spread to those suffering from the life-stultifying effects of domestic violence.

Nine

The Church – A Practical Response

Psalm 72 sets out, in prayer form, a manifesto for a king who was to rule in accordance with the will of God. It refers to a set of social policies which were natural corollaries of the king's position, if he were to be the link between the people and God. The writer asked that God would bestow on the king the qualities and powers necessary for those policies to be implemented. Thousands of years later, the same list could appropriately be adopted as a mission statement for church domestic violence programmes. The psalm reads:

> Endow the king with your justice, O God,
> the royal son with your righteousness.
> He will judge your people in righteousness,
> your afflicted ones with justice.
> The mountains will bring prosperity to the people,
> the hills the fruit of righteousness.
> He will defend the afflicted among the people
> and save the children of the needy;
> he will crush the oppressor . . .
> For he will deliver the needy who cry out,
> the afflicted who have no-one to help.
> He will take pity on the weak and the needy
> and save the needy from death.

He will rescue them from oppression and violence,
for precious is their blood in his sight.
(Psalm 72 :1-4,12–14)

Throughout Scripture we are presented with the picture of God as a loving deity who will intervene in the affairs of humankind to bring justice and healing. However, it should never be forgotten that the Bible does not stop at that point. Undoubtedly, the Lord is the source of such divine qualities as justice and healing, and the fount of power by which evil can be overcome. However, the Christian message does not allow for humans simply to sit back and wait for divine, miraculous intervention. The implementation of the social policies of God's kingdom are to be achieved through the church. The question, then, in relation to domestic violence is: what practical measures can be taken to bring about deliverance from oppression, to end the violence and to bring healing and prosperity to victims?

This chapter sets out a fairly lengthy list of suggestions for specific practical tasks and projects which could be undertaken by a church. It is not meant to be an exclusive list, nor is it suggested that all of the ideas will be suitable for each church. Rather, the list is intended to be a resource of ideas which can be used as starting points for churches looking for ways to help victims. The ideas can be adapted to meet the specific needs of a given community and could simply be used as inspiration for more imaginative or appropriate projects. Prayerful consideration and a wise assessment of local conditions should lead a church in the most appropriate form of services for them.

Throughout this book we have seen how domestic violence is a problem which is woven into the very fabric of our society. We have seen its roots both in the lives and characteristics of individuals and also in our social values and systems. Indeed the combined causation model, developed in chapter 4, demonstrated how all the contributing factors can be drawn together into a pattern which shows clearly how domestic violence is caused and perpetuated. The good news is that there are natural break points in that model. Because domestic violence is a

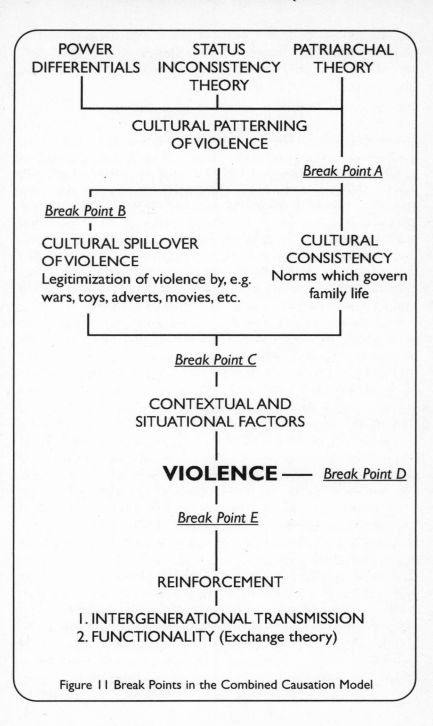

Figure 11 Break Points in the Combined Causation Model

manifestation of sin, it is not invincible. The diagram in this chapter shows the 'weak spots' in the combined causation model, the points at which the following list of practical projects can be targeted.

Break Point A – Tackling cultural values

The diagram shows the first break point at the point where cultural values reinforce domestic violence. Our society is currently structured in such a way that domestic violence is not a shock to society. Violence does not stand out as clearly unacceptable. Rather, it fits in nicely with many of the other attitudes and beliefs held by the community at large. One way to weaken the combined causation model, then, is to challenge these cultural values and so to destroy the cultural consistency theory.

To challenge these values is essentially an extension of general Christian witness. They are challenged, implicitly, in evangelism and Christian teaching and preaching, since many of the values which are to blame for the acceptability of domestic violence are at odds with the gospel. If these values are not wholly at odds with biblical principles, then they tend to be a perversion of Christian teaching. Tackling cultural values can be done at either a micro- or macro-level. Evangelism can happen one-on-one, within the context of personal friendships or work relationships. It can also be accomplished at a much more public level – the Billy Graham-type crusades, with one man speaking to thousands. Likewise, attitudes to cultural values can be changed on an individual level or challenges can be made at an institutional level.

Of course this idea raises all kinds of philosophical issues about the role of the church in politics and the extent to which there can be a 'Christian political agenda'. Such debate is not directly the subject of this book, but one point should be made: Philippians 2 :14-16 talks about the influence of simply living one's own private, everyday life in a godly manner.

> Do everything without complaining or arguing, so that you
> may become blameless and pure, children of God without
> fault in a crooked and depraved generation, in which you
> shine like stars in the universe as you hold out the word of
> life.

The implication is that, by pure example, Christians
demonstrate a more attractive alternative that, by its very
nature, will draw people. That is undoubtedly one form of
influencing society – the 'salt of the earth' approach. 2
Corinthians 5 :20, however, gives a different perspective.
Here Paul is talking about his ministry and uses an
interesting analogy saying, 'We are therefore Christ's
ambassadors, as though God were making his appeal
through us.' An ambassador is a public official, a high-
ranking state official, sent to speak to whole nations as
representative of his or her sovereign or state president. An
ambassador who is entrusted with the task, say, of
persuading Britain to lift trade embargoes against his state,
may well do so on an individual level. He may, on his day
off, meet an Englishman, and through conversation,
persuade him to resume buying his country's oranges in a
supermarket. However, his task will also be performed at a
much higher political level, in that his priority will be the
alteration of governmental policy and changing public
perceptions across the whole land. The church, too, can
bring about the social policies of God's kingdom at both
individual and institutional levels. In relation to domestic
violence there are at least three areas which the church can
tackle.

1. The elimination of sexism

The term sexism here includes patriarchism and gender
domination and control, issues which have been referred to
elsewhere. Orthodox Christianity allows for some debate
about the appropriateness of gender-defined roles, both
within the family and within the church or public life in
general. Individual Christians will have their own views
and it is neither appropriate, nor necessary to enter into
debates here. However, the concern is that any such defined

roles or biblical submission (as discussed in chapter 4) not spill over into subjugation, abuse and oppression. If the latter occurs, the church needs to intervene.

To some extent the church may need to set its own house in order before tackling this issue outside the church doors. How are women treated within the church? Are they dismissed as insignificant, to follow only behind their husbands? Are their concerns, their needs, their safety taken into consideration, or will a cry for help be buried under the cloak of family privacy and male leadership? Are women in the church encouraged to develop their own ministries and careers, or are they banished to make tea?

It is interesting to note that Proverbs 31 :10-31, which sets out the characteristics of a wife of noble character, does not envisage such a woman being a silent, cowering, wholly obedient woman, tied to the church kitchen or nursery. Yes, she cares for her family; she clothes them and cooks and runs the household. However, she is also a landowner with her own trading business. She is also allowed a 'speaking role' and is built up by her husband, not knocked down. She is not hidden in the house but is a publicly-renowned and esteemed character.

> She is clothed with strength and dignity;
> she can laugh at the days to come.
> She speaks with wisdom,
> and faithful instruction is on her tongue . . .
> Her children arise and call her blessed;
> her husband also, and he praises her; . . .
> Give her the reward she has earned,
> and let her works bring her praise at the city gate.

(Proverbs 31 : 25,26,28,31)

The latter phrase is significant, the city gate being the place where the men would gather to do business and, no doubt, to socialize. It is implied that women should be praised and honoured in such company. This praise contrasts with the sexist and degrading conversation which so often takes place in male company today.

The   church   can   play   its   part   in   eliminating discrimination against women simply by influencing the attitudes and conversations of those around them and challenging the common perceptions of women which surface in everyday conversation. However, the church can also contribute to the public debate on women's rights and the need for equal opportunities. Christians can support public campaigns and can even instigate debates on particular instances of sexism.

2. Accelerating changes in law and public policies

To the extent that attitudes and values are necessarily entrenched in the institutions and legal structures of our society, the church can also break the link between those values and violence by entering into the political arena and seeking change in those institutions. For some Christians this may only mean voting one way or another, given the particular policies of a political party at the local or national level. For others it will mean becoming involved with policy-forming bodies. Some will even stand for election as an MP, magistrate or local councillor. Christians can also become involved with community-based initiatives such as policing consultative committees, pressure groups such as the Child Poverty Action Group, or they can actively lobby local or national government.

For example, perhaps increased child-care facilities would help local women work, or perhaps you feel that the local police domestic violence units are understaffed. Pressure at the appropriate point on publicly accountable bodies may have some effect. How many Christians are abreast of proposed legislative changes which may affect this issue? A church may wish to appoint someone responsible for issuing a regular bulletin with material which can equip individuals within the church with the knowledge needed to lobby MPs or other bodies and to pray about specific topics.

Break Point B – Preventing the cultural spillover of violence

The second possible break point is where the general levels of violence in society spill over into the family arena. We have seen in previous chapters how, if violence is common in everyday life, it will not be left at the door of the home like a pair of muddy boots on the doormat. Rather, it will permeate the family as much as every other aspect of culture. Thus one way of breaking the power of domestic violence is to weaken the influence of violence in society in general. This weakening will have the knock-on effect of making violence less common in the resolution of family disputes or in the maintenance of family power differentials. Violence in society can be tackled in a number of ways, and two suggestions are made here.

3. Campaigns against media violence

Violence is found frequently on film and television programmes – whether in children's fantasy cartoons, adult films or news documentaries. It is of some interest that the British Board of Film Classification guidelines allow PG certificates (classed as for general viewing, but with some scenes unsuitable for young children) to be given to films containing 'mild violence'. Even films with a 12 certificate may contain 'more realistic violence, limited in length and intensity', and by the time viewers are fifteen they can be expected to view 'mildly graphic violence and horror with some gore'. Films containing 'graphic violence, providing that it does not encourage sadistic pleasure nor glamourise dangerous weapons' will get an 18 certificate.[1]

There has always been a strong debate in this country about the appropriateness of censorship and the importance of free speech and 'artistic expression'. Christians will have their own views on those issues. However, one does not have to accept censorship to

---

[1] British Board of Film Classification. Quoted in *Television and Censorship*, Donnellan, C. (ed) (Independence 1996)

exercise consumer choice. TV stations and film producers want viewers, and they will cater for the tastes of those who view. Making non-violent preferences known can, therefore, have some influence, however small.

Opinions can be experienced by simple viewing choice. If you don't like it – switch it off! However, Christians can make more specific objections to media violence directly to those with influence. Letters can be sent directly to TV companies. Indeed, during 1992-93 the BBC apparently replied to over one hundred thousand letters and four hundred thousand telephone calls. If the church were to become actively involved in this issue, no doubt those figures would increase massively.

One relevant pressure group is the National Viewers and Listeners Association, made famous by Mary Whitehouse's leadership. The association believes, *inter alia*, that 'violence on television contributes significantly to the increase in violence in society and should be curtailed in the public interest'. Complaints about violence can also be sent to BBC Viewer and Listener Correspondence; for ITV, Channel 4, cable and satellite services, to the Independent Television Commission; for independent radio to the Radio Authority. All complaints can also be sent to the Broadcasting Standards Council. All addresses can be found in Appendix 1.

4. Anti-violence education material / toys

A further issue involves the material which influences young children's perceptions of the world in which they will grow up. Toys are frequently violent in nature – from the traditional toy guns to the more modern space warrior toys. Children's books can also be surprisingly violent in nature. Again, if Christians feel this is an area for concern, action can be taken at a grass-roots level. What toys are available to children in the church nursery and mother and toddler groups? What games are children playing at home or at the homes of their school friends? Play is an important learning process; what lessons are children really learning in what might at first appear to be 'harmless play'?

Action may also be taken at state level. For example, in Australia there is an influential pressure group entitled National Action Against War Toys. This group influenced a national committee dealing with the question of violence in society which reported in 1990, giving recommendations about the control of the toy industry to avoid undue violent influence. In Sweden, as long ago as 1978, negotiations between the Swedish Board for Consumer Policies and the relevant trade organizations resulted in a voluntary agreement that no toys should be sold which related to modern warfare, defined as post-1914. Malta's government has taken steps to prevent the importation of war toys, and the TV advertising of such products has been banned in Greece. These examples show that pressure and consumer opinion which begins at grass-roots level can have results, given time and perseverance.

Break Point C – Dealing with contextual and situational factors

It is at this break point that practical projects can be identified which relate much more directly to domestic violence. These projects may thus be perceived by those wishing to become involved in domestic violence work as being more satisfying and productive. This may well be true, but just as domestic violence is caused by a combination of many factors, so its breakdown will require action at different levels. Thus no programme of action is more important than another. However, the following suggestions are much more people-related and focus on the church giving assistance to specific families who are suffering (or are likely to suffer) from domestic violence.

To the extent that domestic violence is promulgated and reinforced in a given family unit by the pressures and stresses of modern life, as they affect that family, the church can help to relieve those pressures. To the extent that the violence stems from inappropriate coping mechanisms in a particular individual, the church can help him to identify and to deal with conflict and difficulties in a more appropriate manner. All this can be done *ex post facto* by working with families already enmeshed in the web that is domestic violence. However, programmes can also be proactive, seeking to instil non-violent behavioural patterns and expectations before the pressures and tensions build up and the church needs to make a choice about the type of programme which is intended.

5. Realistic expectations

Churches can be guilty of failing to present a realistic picture of life to its young people or new converts. A chorus which is popular at present contains a line stating that as Christians 'all our problems disappear'. Sadly, this is just not true. As Christians we may have access to a great source of support in times of difficulty, but Christians do not sail through life without any problems. This is just as much the case in the family as in any other aspect of Christian life. Nevertheless, church teaching on marriage can present marriage as simply a sugary-sweet, God-decreed institution, the ideal for man and woman, the ultimate plan of God. How many sermons talk about the trials and tribulations of marriage, the financial pressures of keeping a home going, the heartaches of bringing up children, the difficulty of two individuals living as one unit? How often are the topics of childlessness, redundancy, serious illness, divergent ambitions or conflicting family loyalties dealt with by a preacher?

It is all too easy for those with marriage problems to feel that they are doing something wrong, that it is somehow all their fault because they are not living in accordance with the plan of God which would lead them into a blissful union with their spouse. Alternatively, it is all too easy to blame the other spouse, to become resentful because he does not live up to expectations. An unrealistic presentation of marriage within the church thus causes two problems.

Firstly, it colludes with the kind of attitudes and self-views which we have seen forming part of the trap of domestic violence. A victim may feel inadequate and deserving of violence. An abuser may feel things are slipping out of control and that it is his role to ensure, by whatever means, that at least a facade of quiet home life is maintained. Secondly, this unrealistic ideal makes people unlikely to seek help at an early stage. If a struggling couple are able to confide in another Christian couple who will openly share how they resolved the same problems, then that may relieve much of the tension which can lead to an incident of domestic violence. Such openness about the tough realities of marriage will also foster an environment in which victims of violence can seek help from within the church.

The church can thus do much to relieve the contextual and situational factors which lead to domestic violence simply by fostering an environment in which conflict and matrimonial strife can be recognized, and alternative ways of resolving such disputes explored. It is much better for a cry for help from peers to be a norm, rather than being interpreted as an admission of failure to a superior. To some extent, this openness is a prerequisite for any other form of programme directed specifically at victims, since victims will need to feel safe and welcome before opening up to those who wish to help them.

6. Marriage classes

Many ministers hold marriage preparation classes, either for groups or for individual couples. These classes could well be extended as a regular feature of church training schedules to cater not only for engaged couples but also for newly-weds who have had some time to adjust to the realities of marriage, as well as for couples who have been married longer and are coming face-to-face with different problems. Such classes provide an ideal setting in which a clear condemnation of family violence can be given and in which the topic can be discussed openly and in depth. These classes also provide a forum in which interpersonal dynamics can be addressed – an arena in which to examine practical ways of resolving family conflicts. While such classes should have a spiritual content to be of the greatest effect, there should be a strong practical bias also.

7. Parenting classes

An American researcher on domestic violence wrote:

> The implicit models for behaviour provided by government and depicted in the mass media form two legs of the stool supporting American violence. The third leg is the family itself.[2]

Parenting is, in effect, instilling into children a set of values and social mores. How adults act in marriage will, to a large extent, reflect their experiences of family interaction as modelled by their parents. Parenting classes, as a conscious attempt to stop the transmission of domestic violence from generation to generation, in fact fit in well not only under this break point heading, but also under break points A, B and E. Parenting classes have been put in at this stage simply because they relate well to the concept of marriage classes and the church providing a hands-on practical contribution to the family life of its members.

However, parenting issues themselves are closely linked to the situational and contextual factors which can lead to domestic violence. Raising children is a stressful vocation and can cause conflict – both adult-child and inter-adult. Marriage classes may help couples deal with that inter-adult conflict. Parenting classes may help them to avoid that conflict in the first place by teaching them how to coordinate their aims, goals and methods of parenting and to give them an understanding of the roles of each parent. Classes may help to reduce violent methods of dealing with children, e.g. physical chastisement for misdemeanours which could be best dealt with by alternative methods of discipline. Effective parenting can also help to reduce violence between adults (which is inevitably picked up on by children) by removing the cause of the tension which may otherwise give rise to a violent incident.

Following are several very practical ways of reducing some of the situational factors which are commonly

---

[2] Straus, M. and Hotaling, G. *The Social Causes of Husband – Wife Violence* (1979) p.225

associated with domestic violence families.

8. Provision of day-care facilities

Whether a formal nursery placement or an informal playgroup / parents and toddler session, day care can give harassed mothers a break. It also gives them a chance to work, thus increasing their independence (and indirectly, often, their self-worth) whilst at the same time increasing the family budget, which in turn lessens economic pressures on the family. Day care can reduce the isolation of mother and child which is so often a compounding feature of domestic violence. Of course, in providing such care there are practical considerations to bear in mind, such as the issues of cost, qualification for a place and all the usual health and safety regulations. Insurance and training for staff will be needed. However, many churches are now built with child-orientated facilities which can double as an effective outreach programme to families outside the church.

9. Employment

At the time of writing this book, a new Labour government is renewing discussions about the merits of introducing a minimum wage for low earners. Whether or not that ever comes to fruition, financial constraints will continue to be a common situational factor in domestic violence. A minimum wage will only apply to those who work. Mothers with young children will continue to find it hard to obtain work, whilst many men and mothers without children will also have difficulty finding jobs. The minimum wage may well improve matters, but even in families with two good wages, unexpected illness or the needs of a young family can create financial pressures which may lead to violent incidents, if they are not dealt with appropriately.

Many churches feel that they are able to contribute to their community by providing some form of job creation scheme. Such schemes have obvious general benefit and may also, as a side product, help reduce domestic violence incidents. Job creation could include the employment of paid secretaries or cleaners within the church where funds allow. Other schemes have taken advantage of government subsidies or training grants to create jobs which are based in the church but which provide a service to those outside the church. Being able to offer a job, or a training scheme, to a man who is violent in part because of low self-esteem, may be one of the ways in which the church could help to eradicate the violence in his family.

10. Poverty reduction

Job creation is the most obvious way of alleviating poverty and the demoralizing day-to-day dependency on state benefits. However, the church can also use more imaginative ways of poverty alleviation to relieve families from pressure and also be a Christian witness to the families it serves. There are any number of practical programmes which could be initiated, limited only by the imagination of those involved.

Babysitting rotas can allow parents to do casual evening work. Direct food provision can be made – this need not be in the form of 'food parcels' – a network of hospitality which is not expected to be returned in kind can be a godsend to families struggling to provide nutritious meals on a tight budget. To avoid the shaming feeling of being 'charity cases', assistance need not be given but could be 'swapped' for something other than money. Indeed, in some communities entire alternative economic systems have been created. Most people have some talent or practical skill they can provide to others. A system can be devised, amongst a group of people who wish to participate, to value each 'contribution'. So, for example, a church may have a scheme whereby they agree to trade in, say, 'bobbles.' A bobble could be equal to a sum of money so that services could be bought directly, but most importantly, each particular service would be allocated a set number of bobbles by a coordinator. Thus services can be swapped. Perhaps babysitting is valued at one bobble per hour. So, one member may agree to babysit for three hours in return for the invitation to a three-course meal, valued at three bobbles. Or perhaps two hours, or bobbles, worth of plumbing on a wonky washer could be traded for the preparation of a set of CVs and job application letters by someone who has a computer. It must be said that if such a scheme is to be set up it needs some structure, and one must check the tax implications of 'earning' in this way. Nevertheless, such schemes have tremendous potential as a kind of 'human swap shop'. They can make services and goods available to those who could not afford to pay cash, and can give those without a formal job, but with skills, an opportunity to retain self-worth and an alternative to completely unremunerated voluntary work or enforced idleness.

Of course, such a scheme does not remove the added opportunity (obligation?) for giving to those in need without the expectation of reward, where appropriate. However, such schemes could in fact go beyond the removal of the situational facets of poverty. We have seen that domestic violence is supported by cultural norms. One of those norms is to say that the unemployed are useless. That, in turn, leads to an abuser wishing to regain 'status' – he may be useless outside the home but he will be powerful within it. 'Swap shop' schemes have the potential to challenge such cultural norms by showing that the unemployed are not useless at all and have a valued role to play in their community which can be carried out with self-respect.

Break Point D – Limiting the effects of the violence

A fourth break point at which the church can focus its attempts at eradicating domestic violence is by limiting the effects of the violence itself. Programmes at this break point in the model will be the most victim-orientated. For at this break point the focus must be on individual families, to find ways to prevent the reoccurrence of violence or, at the very least, to prevent an escalation of the forms of abuse which are taking place. At this point in the model there is scope for a wide range of programmes, from emergency protection for victims at a time of crisis to the re-establishment of family units.

This type of domestic violence intervention is often the main activity of specialist domestic violence service providers such as Women's Aid. Generally, victims will be helped most by services being expanded rather than repeated, and an overlap in activities between one group and the next will not necessarily be in the victim's best interests. Another consideration is that such support groups are often struggling for finances, operating on a charity basis, with insecure funding. They may have spent much time and effort in establishing their credibility in the community, often having struggled to establish a realistic view of domestic violence within their area. It can make for difficult relations if another agency (especially one just building up experience in domestic violence work) is felt to be in competition with them or is felt to be threatening the relationships which they have built up over time. It makes sense, then, to establish first what services are offered in your area and to take heed of the experience and expertise of those working in this field. The aim should be to cooperate and complement other service providers, not to duplicate their efforts.

That said, there are a whole range of ways in which the church can give very practical assistance to victims of domestic violence. Indeed, some of the suggestions below assume that other services exist and that the church will be working hand-in-hand with other agencies.

11. Information provision

The availability of services for victims of domestic violence varies from area to area. Even in towns where there is good provision, however, victims do not necessarily know about what is available. Ignorance of their true options is one of the reasons victims remain in abusive relationships for so long, and so provision of information is vital if those victims are ever going to escape the violence.

Agencies working with victims – whether state-funded or charities – are often working to a very limited publicity budget. Also, victims may need information from a wide range of agencies – housing, welfare benefits, employment agencies, legal firms and so on. To accumulate all this information demands time and energy – both commodities which an abused woman, perhaps being kept in isolation, may not have. There is therefore opportunity for a church to assist in the provision of information, without necessarily doing any other form of service provision at all. A church could sponsor information packs which collate information from all local services and could assist in making those brochures widely available.

12. Crisis needs of victims

A further problem victims have is obtaining help at the very time when they need it most. With the exception of the police and, very often, Women's Aid groups, most agencies operate only within office hours. On the other hand, a victim may be in great danger at three o'clock in the morning or in the middle of a bank holiday. Some services, such as social services, will have emergency cover, but is there one specialist line or 'drop-in centre' in your area that can give local information to a victim outside of office hours? This really is an extension of information provision, and again, it needs to fit in well with local agencies. However, a church could provide volunteers to train with a local Women's Aid group to help them give a twenty-four-hour service, or they could fund a Freephone out-of-hours telephone line if one does not already exist locally. Or, what about victims who have already begun to seek church help but remain in a dangerous relationship? Perhaps a church could have several trained volunteers who would be available to assist such a victim whenever she should seek help.

13. Refuge accommodation

The available refuge accommodation in Great Britain is well below what is needed to meet the need. Women's Aid refuges work on a national network so that a bed can usually be found out of the area if a local refuge is full. However, that is often far from ideal – particularly where the victim has a job to hold down or children in a local school. Those refuges which do exist can always do with additional support. A church may wish to collaborate with a refuge locally to provide additional services, which could be anything from the donation of good second-hand items to the sponsorship of a refuge worker. Or, a church may wish to go one step further and consider whether there is a need for refuge accommodation in its area which they would be able to meet. This could be on an informal basis, with church members offering accommodation on an emergency basis in their own homes. However, care must be taken when doing that – 'respite' accommodation is one thing, and may be appropriate in certain cases. However, a true refuge offers a level of security and a system of emotional and practical support which accommodation in a friend's house cannot provide. That being the case, a church may even wish to look at running a refuge. Of course, that is a big project and takes a lot of commitment and good research into such issues as health and safety regulations, funding, disabled access, security, links with other referring agencies and the connection with the national network of refuges. A joint project with other agencies would be a way of helping set up a refuge without shouldering all the burden and would be a way of ensuring the necessary expertise was added to the church's willingness to help.

14. Court support services

We saw in a previous chapter just how complex the law is and how many court hearings may be needed for a victim to gain all the remedies open to her. Judges and court staff are, generally, very sympathetic to victims of domestic violence. Nevertheless, the law retains a certain formality, and even witnesses often feel a sense of awe at entering a courthouse for the first time. For victims, it can be ten times worse. They are often ashamed at having to tell the world their story, feeling depressed and anxious generally as a result of the violence and may have the added anguish of having to face their abuser at court. They may simply be nervous about the prospect of using a system which is populated by educated people, some of them wearing strange and old-fashioned garb. They may even be having doubts about the wisdom of taking court action in the first place.

A valuable service, therefore, which can be offered to victims is a 'court support service'. This is often part of Women's Aid work and is a service which a church member could easily offer. It does not require any real knowledge of the legal system as the lawyer running the case should be able to answer all questions a victim may have. However, a basic knowledge of practical things – such as where the toilets are in the local court, where the best bus stop is and where to get a drink – can help a worker put a victim at ease in her surroundings.

A court support worker is really there just to be with a victim, to talk to her in waiting periods, to listen to her fears and, if asked to do so, to find out information for her. Often lawyers will have to leave their clients alone, for example to answer a judge's role call or to talk to the lawyer on the other side. A victim can feel extremely vulnerable when left alone, and having a court support worker there can help enormously. The same applies when she has to leave the building if she is concerned that her abuser or his family may be waiting for her. It is not the role of a court support worker to give the client advice or to tell her what decision to make. A support worker can go into the court hearing only if it is in open court – and many family matters are not. When a court is sitting 'in chambers' a worker can enter the hearing only with the consent of the other side and the permission of the judge. Nevertheless, a worker's support outside the court can be invaluable. The victim can have anyone she likes present in discussion with her lawyer – except certain witnesses – and many lawyers find it helpful to have a supporter with their client as it makes their own job that little bit easier!

15. Counselling / befriending

To some extent counselling has been covered in a previous chapter; suffice it to say again here that in-depth counselling requires specialist training, but there is no reason why a church cannot fund such training for a member to enable the church to offer this service. Befriending is an equally valuable source of support for a victim which does not require formal training but which does require an understanding of the issues surrounding domestic violence and the boundaries between befriending, counselling and giving advice. Again, Women's Aid centres offer this kind of support and are firm that advice should not be given; that is for professionals. However, a friend to visit, to ease the isolation of a victim, to listen to her problems and to assist her in seeking her own solutions, can be the key to a victim gaining the strength she needs to seek help, or to maintain a life away from her abuser.

16. Self-help groups

At the end of the day, victims of domestic violence are not 'cases', 'statistics' or strange examples of a social phenomenon. They are people. Like all others they seek solace and strength in the company of others, particularly those who understand their predicament and have their own experience of violence. Like other sufferers – of cancer or bereavement, for example – victims can gain hope and comfort as well as practical support from self-help groups. A church which is working with a number of victims, or which has links with other agencies doing so, could easily make a room available for such a group to take place and could offer facilities to assist the members, such as refreshments, nursery facilities and publicity. Such groups are helpful in combating the isolating and psychologically debilitating effects of violence by building up the woman's self-confidence and self-worth. Activities can be dictated by the interests and needs of the members. Groups have been known to organize a special day out for children, to have aromatherapy classes or to learn a new craft together. All are simple steps, but vital ones for the victims who need to build new lives with new activities and new friends.

17. Sponsorships

A church may very well feel that there are any number of agencies in the area better qualified to deal with domestic violence than they are. Sponsorship may be an ideal way for the church to assist those agencies without duplicating services or making unqualified attempts to set up new ones. A church could sponsor a room in a refuge or the wages of a Women's Aid worker – children's workers are often badly needed, but unaffordable. Another area ripe for sponsorship is the provision of personal alarms for victims who are most in danger. There are a number of systems on the market, which may be allocated by the police or by social services. One system is an alarm, set up in a house, which allows a victim without a phone to alert the police at once if her abuser returns to the property. Of course, that only operates in the house and so an alternative is for victims to be provided with mobile phones which are programmed only to call emergency numbers. Such facilities are often issued for limited periods of time and on strict conditions so that damage and loss is limited and so that the maximum number of victims can benefit from what are inevitably limited resources. Public funding for the purchase and maintenance of such alarms is often scarce. On the other hand, phones programmed for a limited use are not expensive to run and may be well-suited for church sponsorship.

18. Contact centres

One area in which many churches are already involved is in the provision of contact centres. Contact centres are places in which absent parents can have contact with their children in circumstances where supervision of some sort is needed, or perhaps where no other suitable venue is available. For example, a father may be an alcoholic, and contact is thought desirable for both him and the children but only in an atmosphere where someone can keep an eye on him to ensure he is not drunk or drinking when in charge of the children. Or a father may be seeking contact with a very young baby and there is some genuine doubt as to whether he can care for such a young child alone. The families of contact centre users may have broken down for any number of reasons, but the centres are particularly useful where there has been violence and the victim does not want to come into contact with the abuser and / or there is some concern that he may be violent or emotionally abusive to the children. Obviously, contact centres are a place of last resort (as is supervised contact generally). They are used when there is no family member or friend who can assist with arrangements and when the relationship between the parents has deteriorated to such an extent that they cannot come into contact with each other. In some cases, the centre can be used simply as a neutral venue for the pick-up and collection of the child so the parents do not have to come into contact with each other.

Contact centres are often run on a Saturday and, to be able to offer a safe venue, need a fairly high ratio of trained volunteers to clients. Refreshment facilities are often made available, allowing the centre to make a small profit to cover overheads. It is a matter of policy whether a charge is made for the use of facilities; some accept a one-off donation when clients can afford it, others are free of charge. Some centres will accept self-referrals and referrals directly from other agencies. Others are limited to families who are sent to the centre by the courts or court welfare service. The latter policy has some merit in that it ensures that limited resources are used by those who have been through some kind of vetting process. The disadvantage is that many cases could be settled by lawyers without the case ever having to go to court, if contact centres would accept the family on a solicitor's recommendations.

Centres are intended to be a place of last resort and also a temporary stage, wherever possible. The hope in most cases will be to restart a relationship between parent and child in an atmosphere which provides both security and an opportunity for the absent parent to show that he is able to move away from the centre – to have contact in his own home or to take the child out to the pictures or for the inevitable McDonald's hamburger. Churches are often well-placed to offer contact centres, frequently having a number of people who are able to work with children and families on a rota basis, and having rooms suitable for children which may otherwise only be used for Sunday schools. Churches interested in such a project would be well advised to contact the National Centre of Contact Centres – see Appendix 1 for the address – which offers support and training.

19. Safety plans

Safety plans are written plans which help a victim to focus on keeping herself and her dependants safe from violence. Such a plan may list the places to which she can go when violence occurs or places where she can leave money in cases of emergency. Appendix 2 contains a sample safety plan. The use of a safety plan can help a victim act rationally in time of great danger and stress, when she may otherwise be unable to think logically or to take the best action. A safety plan is one simple thing which church members can do with victims who seek their help. They are low-cost but may be highly effective in assisting a victim.

20. Coordination of services

One problem faced in many areas is that all the services available to victims may be dispersed between several offices and centres, often over a great distance, all with their own offices, hours and procedures for giving out information. Victims may have to ride a merry-go-round of bus trips, queues and repetitive interviews before they are able to obtain all the information they need to make a decision about their future. If services can be coordinated so they are available from one centre – or, at the least if *information* about the services is available from one centre

– then several benefits follow. Victims do not become discouraged or confused. Agencies often become more aware of what others are doing and service gaps can then be closed and duplication avoided. More importantly, misunderstandings between agencies about the role of other service providers can be prevented. There is a great risk, where there is little coordination, of, say, a policeman telling a victim to get a Power of Arrest attached to her injunction where none is available to her, or of a solicitor telling a victim that she will have to wait on the housing list, because of lack of awareness of the existence of a refuge or emergency housing rules.

The ideal form of coordination is perhaps the establishment of a 'one shop stop', where each relevant agency can have a representative available to advise victims under the one roof. Or, key workers could be trained to give out accurate information at all agencies and services, although they actually work for the centre. The major problem in achieving this is, again unsurprisingly, funding. Staff may be volunteers, although in practice at least some full-time, professional staff are needed to give a quality service. Also a building is needed – preferably somewhere unobtrusive and 'disguised' so that if a victim is seen going into the centre it is not immediately apparent why she is there.

A church may be able to provide such a venue, especially if they offer other day-time activities such as mother and toddler groups or a coffee bar which would provide a 'decoy'. Obviously such a project again requires cooperation both with and from all the other agencies in the area. An alternative form of coordination is to keep each agency aware of the activities of the others. Most agencies now refer to others and it can be extremely useful to know, for example, that Women's Aid often offers free counselling or that the local contact centre now operates on a self-referral basis. A church which has the goodwill of all agencies in the area may be able to offer assistance to them all by organizing and facilitating an inter-agency forum for regular 'update' meetings or by undertaking the preparation of an inter-agency newsletter. Such projects may seem removed from direct work with victims, but by ensuring that full and accurate information reaches victims, by one means or another, the church would be improving the service given to victims and would thus enhance the victim's chance of first escaping the violence and then rebuilding her life in a non-violent atmosphere.

21. Rebuilding of family units

Many of the projects suggested above focus either on general social policies or else on emergency protective measures. But what of family units which are left once the violence is identified, the abuser's behaviour condemned as unacceptable and the victim's immediate safety secured? Is the dismantling of violent relationships all that can be offered? The church can play a vital role in the rebuilding of those family units where both parties are willing to participate in a learning process. Non-violent dynamics can be substituted for violent reactions, but such a restructuring of the relationship requires long-term support. It is about more than simply telling an abuser not to hit his partner and letting the victim know that she has alternatives to remaining in a violent home. One researcher, considering the effect of removing violence from a relationship, concluded:

> equality will reduce or eliminate certain kinds of conflict but at the same time it will create new conflicts . . . . consequently a reduction in the level of violence also requires that couples have interpersonal skills and conflict management skills needed to cope with and realise the benefits of a less rigid family system.[3]

In other words, families need to get used to living without violence. They need to be taught the alternatives. The church can contribute immensely to this process, be it by individual pastoral counselling, group marriage classes or the 'befriending and mentoring' of a couple by one or two couples with experience in resolving relationship problems.

---

[3] ibid. p.225

At times it will be necessary for a family to be split up to achieve bodily and emotional safety for victims. However, such a response to domestic violence does run against Christian teaching on the sanctity of marriage and the family. By offering positive encouragement and practical assistance to families seeking to rebuild from the rubble caused by domestic violence, the church can offer a full 'package' of assistance which is in accordance with the gospel message of restoration and healing. Of course, such aspects of the Christian message have to be taken up by those to whom they are on offer. The church cannot force an abuser to work through the violence, nor can it force a victim to try and save a relationship in which she experienced pain and suffering. Nevertheless, by the saving grace of God such reconciliation and renewal is available, and this is one area in which the church is intrinsically better equipped than any other social agency to offer guidance and encouragement.

Break Point E – Preventing the reinforcement of existing violence

The fifth point at which the model of combined causation can potentially be broken is at the stage where existing violence is reinforced. This strategy has three aspects. Firstly, the cost of the violence to abusers can be increased, so that violence which may just have started will not become entrenched. Secondly, work can be done with the second generation, so that violence does not become an inherited way of life for the children of victims and abusers. Thirdly, attempts can be made to prevent violence being reinforced in society as a whole. Of course, the latter relates back to break point A, dealing with cultural values. Given that the pattern of violence is circular, it should come as no surprise that the solutions feed back into each other in a continual cycle from general societal values through the individual family and out into the wider social arena again. There are several ways in which the reinforcement of existing violence can be tackled.

22. Increasing the costs in the church

In chapter 4 we looked at how the exchange theory of violence holds that abusers are violent because the benefits outweigh the disadvantages. Increasing the costs of violence should, if that theory holds true, contribute to a decline in the use of violence. The church itself can increase the costs. What costs does the church impose for abusers? Is violence tacitly condoned by embarrassed 'sweeping under the carpet', or is there strong denouncement of an abuser's actions and pressure put on him to change his ways? Does violence in the home preclude an abuser from activities in the church, or are veiled hints about his behaviour contradicted by his continued participation in church functions? Of course, there is a world of difference between discipline and ostracizing, but if the church is to discipline its members, then just as with small children, rules must be backed up by appropriate sanctions if they are to be effectual.

23. Increasing the costs in society

To the extent that the church is a part of society and, ideally, a positive influence upon it, it is only a logical step from the last point for the church to look outwards and attempt to increase the costs of violence in society as a whole. Again, there is a strong link here to the suggestions made under break point A.

24. Education

If the next generations are to be saved from domestic violence, education must be a strong part of any campaign. Children need to consider at an early age such issues as gender roles, relationship dynamics and conflict resolution, if their own relationships are to be conducted with a non-violent ethos. Violence, as we have seen, is often closely linked to assumptions and beliefs about 'women's jobs' or 'men's rights'. Education, both informal and formal, can be vital in enabling children to challenge the perceptions and expectations they may have picked up from observing violent parents or other adults.

Churches are often able to participate in school assemblies or religious education classes, where a programme designed around relationships may be well placed. However, there are ample opportunities for education within the church in youth groups and Sunday schools. Imaginative use can be made of drama, music and other media to get the message across in a friendly and acceptable way.

25. Children's work

Previous suggestions for action, in so far as they have been directly victim-orientated, have largely been aimed at adults. Children's work is, however, just as important. Children who have witnessed violence, or who have experienced it themselves, generally need help to work through that experience. Self-blame, fear, shame, loss of self-confidence, confusion – all these are just a few of the emotions which child victims can experience. At a simple level, a befriending scheme for children to mirror that for adults, as suggested above, but tailored for the needs of children, would perhaps go some way to meeting needs. To have a non-violent adult role model, or a friend in whom they could confide their fears and distress without 'making Mummy upset' could prevent a child from internalizing emotions and letting them lie unresolved.

Of course, other children will need more specialist help – child counselling, play therapy or even specialist psychological or psychiatric help. The church could support members who have such professional qualifications or could perhaps sponsor appropriate service providers to make such services for children more widely available. Children's work has the dual effect of dealing with the damage already done to vulnerable young people and also giving them a positive new start in life, preventing their own lives from mirroring those of their parents.

26. Divorce information provisions

Domestic violence often leads to a divorce. The potential for the effects of the violence being reinforced and for power battles between parents is great when bitter divorce proceedings take place. Divorce is a seriously disruptive event for any child to cope with, but it can be much less damaging if care is taken to ensure the child is as informed as his age and emotional maturity demands, that he is not ignored by distracted parents or used as a pawn in their disagreements. A child may have some emotional turmoil and some questions which arise from the violence. Those issues can either be dealt with and set aside so that the child can go on happily to the next stage in his life, or they can be left to fester and deepen as the child's needs are ignored whilst matrimonial disputes rage. The way adults handle events consequent to a family split may even cause the child further damage which will compound his existing difficulties.

The church may play a role in preventing this form of reinforcement of the effects of domestic violence by providing family members with information and guidance during a divorce or the cessation of cohabitation. To do this is not necessarily to condone the divorce, but it does require an acceptance that the divorce is inevitable and that the church can step in and minimize the subsequent damage. Chapter 5, on legal issues, mentions the formal 'information meetings' which must be provided under the new divorce legislation and it may be possible for a church to become involved as a provider of those meetings. A church may not wish to do so on such a public basis however, when there would not be any personal connection with those seeking a divorce, and so no opportunity to encourage reconciliation before the decision to divorce is made. However, the church can still provide information as an adjunct to the formal information meeting, or as an additional service for couples who have not married and thus can split up without coming under the legislative provisions. Information provision here is intended to mean – either exclusively, or *inter alia* – information about the effects of domestic violence and family breakdown on the children, and how such effects can be avoided or minimized. Parents who cause their children emotional damage in such situations are not necessarily selfish or uncaring parents but may be acting out of ignorance or misconceptions. For example, some mothers refuse contact to a father, genuinely believing that the child would be better off without reminders of the past when, in fact, the body of expert opinion holds that it is most important for a child to maintain a relationship with both parents. Again, information provision demands training and experience, but not necessarily at a level which could not be acquired by a volunteer within a church, particularly if local agencies were willing to offer training to a church team.

There are a myriad of ways in which a church can help victims who are currently suffering from domestic violence and in which the church can contribute to the eradication of violence in society as a whole. Other projects will no doubt evolve as concerned people read this and other books and carefully consider how they can best become involved, given the existing service provision in their areas. Dealing with domestic violence is not an easy vocation. It is both stressful and, at times, distressing. It demands commitment and energy from those who choose to become involved in the field. However, there is a great need in our society at present for those who are prepared to sacrifice time and resources to help victims. Victims are amongst the most needy and desperate individuals in our communities – but they are also the most invisible. Each small effort which is made to help can have a huge effect on the lives of victims and their children. It is a challenge which is open to each and every church. What about you? Will you help?

Conclusion

Karen was one of my clients. She was thirty-two and had four children by the time she came to see me. Her story as told to me went something like this:

I got used to seeing Dad belt my Mum when he was in a bad mood. Johnny [her brother] and I just used to get out of the way. He wasn't so bad with us and I thought it was all quite normal. I wouldn't have said I was unhappy, but looking back I was. I would spend as much time at friends' houses as I could – anything to get away from his yelling. I suppose that was why I was so keen to get married. I met Davey when I was seventeen and we married when I was just eighteen. I was pregnant by nineteen, with the second one coming two years later. It was when I wanted to go out to work that it all went wrong. He started to hit me too. I was in hospital a few times – broken wrist and concussion, that kind of thing. But he was good to the kids, and it wouldn't have been any better going back home. I was with him for seven years.

Then he got caught up with a bad crowd at the pub and he ended up doing a robbery and got sent down. It was hard with the kids on my own but after a while I realized I wasn't afraid any more. Then after two years I met another bloke – Jed. He was actually from London – he was working up here and my friend had met him in a club and had gone out with him a few times. Then she split up with him – we had a drink together and she complained that he was a bit controlling, wanting to know where she was, that kind of thing. To me, that just sounded like he cared about her. Davey couldn't give two hoots what I was up to.

I started seeing Jed and then Davey found out and wanted a divorce and the house sold. He was due to be coming out soon and I was scared, so when Jed insisted we move back to London with him I agreed. That was the worst decision I made because he was just the same. I couldn't move without explaining to him what was going on. We had another two kids and the violence started when I was pregnant. Now my eldest boy has threatened to call the police – not for his Dad, but to ask them to arrest me for not doing something to stop it – they are so scared.

You would think I'd know better after my Dad, but I never seem to see it coming. I'll never trust another man again.

Karen's story is an excellent example of the phenomenon of repeat victimization. It appears from crime figures that many victims of crime – including domestic violence – are victims many times over. In domestic violence that may mean many assaults within one relationship or several violent relationships. Repeat victimization compounds the distress and despair felt by victims. Living with violence is not a bad event which they can learn to forget – it becomes a lifestyle of no alternative.

The church is perhaps the best-placed of all agencies to bring a message of hope to victims. It can intervene in practical ways to rescue a victim from violence. It can show examples of how relationships can be non-violent and how marriage can be a good institution. It can help to bring about the eradication of violence, both for that victim and in society as a whole. However, it also has a unique message, which only the church can impart.

The church may not be able to enforce the criminal laws against assault. It may not be able to provide advice on injunctions and divorce. It may not even be able to provide such a wide range of social provision as Women's Aid organizations or social services. However, it can bring the powerful and effective Word of God into the situation. It can relay to a victim the compelling promises of hope and healing. Other agencies may be able to offer a new start in life, a relocation, a break from old ties. But only the church can offer salvation and a totally new life in Christ. The church is called to deliver this message to all mankind – domestic violence victims included.

Appendix 1 -
USEFUL ADDRESSES

BBC
(British Broadcasting Corporation)
Radio and Head Office
Broadcasting House,
Portland Place,
London,
W1A 1AA

Tel : 0171 580 4468

Broadcasting Standards Council
5 – 8 The Sanctuary,
London,
SW1P 3JS

Tel: 0171 233 0544

Childline
2nd Floor,
Royal Mail Building,
Studd Street,
London.
N1 OQW

Tel : 0171 239 1000

Families Need Fathers
Administration Office,
134, Curtain Road,
London,
EC2A 3AR

Tel : 0171 613 5060
Information Line: 0181 886 0970

Independent Television Commission (ITC)
33, Foley Street,
London,
W1P 7LB

Tel : 0171 255 3000

ITV Network Centre
200, Grays Inn Road,
London,
WC1X 8HF

Tel : 0171 843 8000

MATCH
Mothers Apart From their Children,
c/o BM Problems,
London.
WC1N 3XX

The Men's Centre
A men's counselling service on domestic violence
Tel : 0171 267 8713

MAPP (Merseyside Abusive Partner's Project)
Based at St. Helens Women's Aid
Tel : 01744 – 454290

National Viewers' and Listeners' Association (NVALA)
All Saints House,
High Street,
Colchester
CO1 1UG

Tel : 01206 561155

NCH Action For Children
85, Highbury Park,
London,
N5 1UD

Tel : 0171 226 2033

Newnham Asian Women's Project
PO Box 225,
London,
E7 9AA

Tel : 0181 472 0528

Northern Ireland Women's Aid Federation
129, University Street,
Belfast,
B17 1HP

Tel : 01232 249041 / 249358

NSPCC Child Protection Helpline
Tel : 0800 800 500

NSPCC
National Society for the Prevention of Cruelty to Children
National Centre,
42, Curtain Road,
London,
EC2A 3NH

Tel : 0171 825 2500

Refuge
PO Box 855,
Chiswick,
London,
W4 4JF

Tel : Office – 0181 747 0133
Tel : 24-hour crisis line – 0181 995 4430

The Save the Children Fund
17, Grove Lane,
London,
SE5 8RD

Tel : 0171 703 5400

Scottish Women's Aid
12, Torpichen Street,
Edinburgh,
EH3 8JQ

Tel : 0131 221 0401

SOLAS ANOIS
Irish Women's Domestic Violence Project

Tel : 0181 664 6089

Victim Support National Office
Cranmer House,
39, Brixton Road,
London,
SW9 6DZ

Tel : 0171 735 9166

Victim Support Scotland
14, Frederick Street,
Edinburgh,
EH2 2HB

Tel : 0131 225 7779

Victim Support Republic of Ireland
Room 16,
29/30 Dane Street,
Dublin 2

Tel : 00353 16798673

Welsh Women's Aid National Offices
12, Cambrian Place, Aberystwyth,
Dyfed,
SY23 1NT

Tel : 01970 612748

26, Wellington Road,
Rhyl,
Clwyd,
LL18 1BN

Tel : 01745 334767

38/48, Crwys Road,
Cardiff,
CF2 4NN

Tel : 01222 390874

Women's Aid Federation England Ltd.
PO Box 391,
Bristol,
BS99 7WS

National Helpline : 0117 963 3542

Appendix 2 –
SAFETY PLAN

A safety plan can help a victim plan ahead to prepare her for action in a time of emergency. Making such advance plans, perhaps with the assistance of a friend or support worker, can help a victim to realize that it is possible for her to help herself and that she is not as trapped as she perhaps at first thought. When the time to implement the plan comes, having simple steps written down can help a victim to concentrate and to take logical steps, despite the pain and fear she may feel. Safety plans should be revised on a regular basis as the needs of a victim change – for example she may move into different property or her neighbour who helps her may move away. Also regular revision helps to keep the contents of the plan fresh in a victim's mind.

Safety plans can be drafted to the needs of each individual, or they can be a standard form which each organization produces. The example below is a short version for the purposes of an example only. A longer version, adapted from one published on the Internet by the Nashville Police Department is to be found in the author's book *Domestic Violence: Picking up the Pieces* (Lion 1997).

1. Dealing with the violence

1. The best way to leave my house in an emergency is ....

2. I will keep a bag filled with things I would need in an emergency at

....

3. The best place to go in an emergency for help is ....

An alternative is ....

4. If my children are witnesses to the violence I will teach them to

....

5. I can ask my neighbour .... to phone the police if she / he hears sounds of an assault coming from my house.

6. Good ways to placate my partner are...

7. Good ways to defend myself and minimize injuries are

....

2. Making myself less of a victim

1. I will improve my physical safety in my house by................................

2. I will leave emergency clothes and money with..................................

3. I will ask ....and .... if I could stay with them if I have to leave my home.

4. I will save some money for emergencies by ....

5. I will phone the following people if I feel in danger or if I need help:

Name	Telephone Number
....	....
....	....

6. I will make a bag up for emergencies containing the following items:

....

7. I will make enquiries with the following people about leaving my partner:

....

Index